Women Who Dare to Dream

ILLUMINATION
PUBLISHERS

Women Who Dare to Dream

Shawn E. Patterson

Dreams really do come true.

Women Who Dare to Dream

Copyright © 2013 by Shawn E. Patterson

Printed in the United States of America

ISBN: 978-1-939086-02-0

Unless otherwise indicated, all Scripture references are from the *Holy Bible, New International Version*, Copyright 1973, 1978, 1984, 2011 by the International Bible Society. Used by permission of Zondervan Bible Publishers.

Additional translations used: Scripture quotations taken from the *Amplified® Bible*, copyright © 1954, 1958, 1962, 1964, 1965, 1987 by The Lockman Foundation. Used by permission. (www. Lockman.org). *Holy Bible, New Living Translation* copyright © 1996, 2004, 2007 by Tyndale House Foundation. Used by permission of Tyndale House Publishers Inc., Carol Stream, Illinois 60188. All rights reserved. New Living, NLT, and the New Living Translation logo are registered trademarks of Tyndale House Publishers. Scripture quotations taken from the *New American Standard Bible®*, copyright © 1960, 1962, 1963, 1968, 1971, 1972, 1973,1975, 1977, 1995 by The Lockman Foundation. Used by permission. (www.Lockman.org). *The Holy Bible, New King James Version®*. Copyright © 1982 by Thomas Nelson, Inc. All rights reserved. Scriptures taken from the *Contemporary English Version* © 1991, 1992, 1995 by American Bible Society, used by permission. Scripture quotations from *The Holy Bible, English Standard Version®* (ESV®), copyright © 2001 by Crossway, a publishing ministry of Good News Publishers. Used by permission. All rights reserved. *New Revised Standard Version Bible*, copyright 1989, Division of Christian Education of the National Council of the Churches of Christ in the United States of America. Used by permission. All rights reserved. *THE MESSAGE: The Bible in Contemporary Language*. Copyright © 2002 by Eugene H. Peterson. All rights reserved. *THE MESSAGE* Numbered Edition copyright © 2005. Scripture quotations marked (NIrV) are taken from the *Holy Bible, New International Reader's Version®, NIrV®*. Copyright © 1995, 1996, 1998 by Biblica, Inc.™ Used by permission of Zondervan. All rights reserved worldwide.

Cover and interior design: Toney C. Mulhollan

About the author: Shawn E. Patterson is a devoted wife and mother, as well as a passionate women's ministry leader, mentor and motivational speaker. She has devoted over twenty-three years of her life encouraging, teaching and training diverse women of all ages to build an intimate relationship with God and embrace his dream for their lives. Her dynamic and down-to-earth style is both refreshing and inspiring. She enjoys traveling throughout the US and abroad sharing her life and speaking at women's programs and conferences. She and her husband, Michael, recently celebrated their twenty-third anniversary and together they have two children, Alexis and Joseph. Michael and Shawn have served in the full-time ministry as evangelist and women's ministry leader since 1990, first in the New York City Church of Christ and currently in the Greater Atlanta Church of Christ. Together they are experienced and effective in ministering to people in various stages of life. Since the Pattersons became Christians in 1985 as college students, they have shared a deep conviction and commitment to passing the torch of leadership to the next generation!

Contents

Dedication

To my heart and my hero, my mom: You fought the good fight.

I have fought the good fight, I have finished the race, I have kept the faith. Now there is in store for me the crown of righteousness, which the Lord, the righteous Judge, will award to me on that day—and not only to me, but also to all who have longed for his appearing. (2 Timothy 4:7–8)

Acknowledgements

I would like to express my gratitude to everyone who has been a part of making my dream become a reality. Writing this book was an exciting adventure and took a team of individuals who were devoted to the journey. It would not have been accomplished without them and the many people who have prayed and encouraged me along the way. I am indebted to my husband, Mike, for his inspiration, loving support, and the example he set of becoming an author himself. I am thankful for my precious children, Alexis and Joe, for being my biggest fans and for Mama BJ always believing I could do anything. I appreciate all the encouragement of the Greater Atlanta Church of Christ and I am so grateful for all the courageous sisters who trusted me to tell their powerful stories. I also want to thank my editor at Illumination Publishers, Amy Morgan, for her relentless dedication to this project and for her capable assistance, guidance, and clever suggestions. She gets me. Also, it has been a pleasure to work with all the wonderful people at Illumination Publishers. Their expertise and professionalism have been invaluable to me.

Above all, I thank God for opening this door as another way to make his name glorious.

Foreword

I have the most vivid memory of Shawn as a young Christian and young leader. She was passionate beyond belief, and her laughter was the most amazing and contagious thing in the world. At every baby shower or bridal shower, every party, every devotional or service that I would walk into, I could always hear Shawn's laugh, and wherever she was, that part of the room was electric…and happy. She was this little person but her presence was enormous.

I remember Mike and Shawn going to Harlem to lead that part of our congregation and how much they were needed. As they would prove over and over again, they were the right ones for the job. They did great. Shawn had both older women and younger women to work with, and she was very young herself, but the standard she set for herself and those she worked with was so high and so clear. She really loved people and had a vision for everyone she came in contact with. She had a dream for a church centered on Jesus and, along with Mike, worked tirelessly and successfully to see that dream fulfilled many times.

They heard the call to leave Harlem and go to the Bronx, and again, they flourished. You'd never know how hard a time Shawn had growing up, and she did overcome adversity, but what impresses me and what I admire is how kind and compassionate she has always been, and how joyful.

In the years leading up to 2003, we had nearly 6000 members of the New York City church divided into five groups lead by five couples; Mike and Shawn were one of those couples, and I came to depend on her so much. When things got really hard in 2003 and 2004 and our hearts were broken, Shawn was one of the friends who showed up for me. After twenty-one years of leading the church in NYC, Steve and I had moved to Savannah, and Shawn was one of the first ones to come just to see me. We encouraged one another to persevere, to be compassionate…and to forgive. She pushed me to keep on and not give up, even though she had been so hurt herself.

Along with Mike, Shawn has always loved and taken care of my husband's family as they have aged and faced their challenges. In every way, she is family. She is my sister and she is my friend.

Shawn is an honorable woman. Her integrity is unquestionable. I've watched her face down adversities of many kinds: church drama, racism, health issues…I think about how self-denying she has been; how self-denying she always is. When treated unkindly she is kind. When dealt unfairly she is forgiving. And always, always she is gracious.

She's done it all: trained women for the ministry and for life, had a successful marriage, raised children; and when times were tough even sold real estate! But one thing has always been for certain with this wonderful woman: Shawn has always been clear and passionate about the ministry and the purpose of the church and its people. In fact, in times of chaos, Shawn has always been an oasis. In times of confusion, Shawn has been fruitful. In times of loneliness in my life, Shawn has been there for me.

When I was diagnosed with lymphocytic lymphoma, she was one of the few people who just said, "We're coming to see you right now!" and then Mike and she flew themselves out and showed up at our door. All she said was, "I just have to look into your eyes!" That still makes me cry...

She's exceptional and has a lot of friends; she's helped a lot of people dream. She creates a loving fellowship in every ministry she starts, every ministry she leads. Where the Pattersons are, you can count on inspiring services, loving fellowship, and always growing numbers, because they are always building. She exudes a zeal that infects anyone who comes into her orbit.

Shawn says she's grateful to me for inspiring her to dream. I don't know about that; I only know that she has inspired me to never stop dreaming and I can promise you, if you let her, she will help you to dream. With her influence, you can hardly escape becoming one of the women who dare to dream.

—Lisa Johnson

Tribute to My Mom

This book, my first, is a tribute to the most remarkable woman I have ever known: my mother, Betty Jean Reid (affectionately known as BJ or Mama BJ). Mom was born in Brooklyn, New York on February 2, 1936 and was the daughter of Hortense Edith Francis and Charles Richardson. She was raised at 416 East 129th Street, Harlem, NY.

As I have evolved as a woman, my appreciation for my mom has grown profoundly. I will forever treasure her, God's precious gift to me, and admire all the good that was in her.

From birth, Mom faced seemingly insurmountable challenges, defying all odds. After she passed, I discovered that she had been adopted by the wonderful woman I knew as my grandma, Ms. Oakley, and never knew her biological mother or father. There is no record of the adoption, so the details of how Mom got to Ms. Oakley will remain a mystery to me, but ultimately I believe it was all God. Mom chose never to speak of it or make it an issue in her life because she was so grateful and undoubtedly loyal to Ms. Oakley, who worked as a beautician and also cleaned houses in order to afford things like piano lessons for Mom.

Mom was a consummate musician. She never bragged about the fact that she was a child prodigy, a classical concert pianist at age three. She also had the honor of performing at Steinway Music Hall, and her picture appeared in the *New York Amsterdam News*. She was a gifted poet and songwriter and wrote songs for a few of the popular men's groups of her day. Most endearing of all were the poems, lullabies and songs she wrote and sang to my brother, Jay, and me.

As a child, Mom learned that she would have to be a persistent fighter. She was born deaf in one ear and before age five lost most of her hearing in the other ear due to scarlet fever. She also went blind in one eye because of an unknown disease that we now realize was glaucoma and curable if she had had better care. Her classmates who enjoyed harassing her because of her disabilities cruelly bullied Mom, but Ms. Oakley taught her how to be brave. I recall Mom telling me that Ms. Oakley challenged her to stand up for herself. "So, what are you going to do? Are you going to sit in the house and feel sorry for yourself or are you going to go out there and show them that you are not afraid of anything and you can do just what they can do, only better?" Ms. Oakley taught Mom some invaluable lessons that would carry her through life: Never make excuses for your physical challenges, because God made up for them by giving you gifts, and never ever feel sorry for yourself or give up. After one of her talks with Ms. Oakley, Mom was ready when four girls approached her and one threw a brick at her that hit her in the stomach. Mom took a deep breath, put up her fists, and fought all four girls. Let's just say that those girls never bothered her again.

Adulthood ushered in even more harrowing challenges. Mom's physical health continued to decline as she became legally blind and continuously lost hearing in her scarlet-fever-damaged ear. As far back as I can remember, she suffered with severe asthma attacks almost daily. It was terrifying to watch, but she handled them with ease and never complained. She actually expressed thankfulness to God for what she did have. She continually adjusted, and she laughed at herself when she misheard something. Mom had an uncanny ability to be content with very little.

With that indomitable spirit and amicable sense of humor, my mom, an ordinary woman, made some extraordinary accomplishments. She not only victoriously lived with several chronic illnesses, she also remained loyal to my dad, Joe, for thirty-five years through his addiction and through good and bad times. With God's help, she triumphantly overcame her own alcohol addiction and the demons that accompanied it.

Through all of the highs and lows, I am convinced that love never fails. During the last decade of Mom's life, what may have started with a single seed of love flourished into a bountiful garden overflowing with the exceedingly beautiful fruits of the Spirit. I thank God that on May 19, 2010 at seventy-four years old, Mama BJ humbled herself before God in the waters of baptism and received what she craved for her whole life: a true relationship with her Lord and Savior.

Finally, Mom would fight her last formidable foe. After suffering with gut-wrenching pain for several months, in March 2011 she was diagnosed with advanced pancreatic cancer. It was aggressive, extremely painful, and deadly.

I must confess that I was a little upset with God for a minute. I wondered, if Mom had to be sick with cancer, why did it have to be one of the most painful, worst types of cancer? I also struggled with God's timing. We had just thrown my mom a big birthday celebration and she was on cloud nine. She sweetly told me it was one of the happiest times of her life. We were just beginning to have the friendship I'd always prayed for. God would gently remind me that his ways are higher than my ways and his thoughts are higher than my thoughts. I was going to have to dig deep and learn to trust in him with every detail and not lean on my own understanding.

In typical Betty Jean style, she faced this incomprehensible disease with her unshakeable faith, audacious courage, and patient endurance. She set an example of how to patiently endure suffering as she waited for God to rescue her.

How inspiring it was for me to talk with her in her last weeks, hearing her speak of her love for God and her gratitude that he would be with her no matter what happened. What a joy it was to pray with her and hear all of God's words she had committed to memory and was clinging to. It was mind-blowing to witness the courage Mom displayed throughout the whole dying process. When her physicians told her that chemo would most likely not work at all in her case, she was determined to try, mainly because she had promised my daughter, Alexis, that she would be at her graduation in May. Mom kept her promise, traveling by plane from New York to Atlanta in excruciating pain, in a wheel chair and barely able to stand.

Until the end of time, I will cherish the memories of serving Mom during the last five months of her life, and they will forever be engraved on my heart. It was her desire to be cared for at home as long as possible, so my brother and I were determined to do that. We were blessed to have the help of Jay's fiancé, the grandkids, and the mighty hospital ministry in the Bronx. Mom was superindependent, so she did as much as she could for herself as long as she could—and then she gave us specific instructions on how to take care of her! It was one of the supreme privileges of my entire life.

Although during the last days of her life she suffered tremendous agony, they were her finest hours, made up of unforgettable moments. Family and close friends surrounded her, and we enjoyed moments of healing, connecting with God and one another, singing, prayer, and intimate talks. One night as I was sitting by her bedside, Mom asked me, "So, what are we going to do when I can't talk anymore and tell you-all what I need?" I said, "Well, I'll just have to ask you, and you'll have to blink or squeeze my finger." Then on Wednesday, July 27, the time came for her to say her good-byes. Mama BJ called Jay, the grandkids, and me into her room one at a time to express her love and special wishes for each of us. The next day Mom could no longer talk and needed to go to hospice, where she lost consciousness. The hospice staff was another gift from God to our family. One nurse mentioned that when the body dies, some healthcare professionals believe that hearing is the last thing to go, so I lay next to Mom, played soft music, talked to her, kissed her, and told her I loved her, over and over. Amazingly, with the little strength she had left she squeezed my hand and tried to blink. She died in my arms on July 31, 2011.

I have a gazillion things to be grateful for, and I feel so unworthy.

I can only thank God and praise him for making my mom, shaping her, changing her, and saving her. I pray that God will forgive me for the times when I took her for granted, was embarrassed by her or ashamed of her, and did not tell her enough that I was proud of her.

I had a mom who decided to live well and who loved the people in her life relentlessly. I had a mom who with every fiber of her being loved my brother and me unconditionally (it's so funny: we couldn't tell who was the favorite). I had a mom who was loyal to the core and was my husband's and my biggest fan. I had a mom who selflessly sacrificed what she needed so that we could have what we wanted. I had a mom who humbly and constantly served those around her. I had a mom who showered everyone around her with thoughtful cards and gifts. I had a mom who called me almost every day to encourage me and tell me she loved me. I had a mom who loved my kids and whom my kids loved more than words can say. I had a mom who was kindhearted and giving to family, friends, and strangers alike. I had a mom who was inspired by the love of God's church and who inspired many with her persevering and uncompromising joy.

Betty Jean displayed to us the power of one ordinary life. Her humble home and her neighborhood full of loyal neighbors and friends remained her favorite place to be on earth with her family. What mattered most to her were the people God put in her life to love and be loved by. Her simple life left a legacy and made an impact on many because she loved well and in the end, she died well. That is why this book is dedicated to my mom, my hero.

Introduction

God Is the Divine Dreamer

God loves with a great love the man whose heart is bursting with a passion for the impossible. —William Booth

"No eye has seen, no ear has heard,
and no mind has imagined
what God has prepared
for those who love him." (1 Corinthians 2:9 NLT)

We have all heard this warning: "You never get a second chance to make a good first impression." Naturally, every author wants to make a good first impression—and rightfully so. Therefore, it was my desire to begin my first book with the spotlight and focus on our Almighty God. It is only in him and through him that I have the opportunity to experience becoming an author, which is yet another of his dreams for me fulfilled!

Dreaming Begins with the Beginning—GOD

O LORD, you have examined my heart
and know everything about me.
You know when I sit down or stand up.
You know my thoughts even when I'm far away.
You see me when I travel
and when I rest at home.
You know everything I do.
You know what I am going to say
even before I say it, LORD.
You go before me and follow me.

You place your hand of blessing on my head.
Such knowledge is too wonderful for me,
   too great for me to understand!
I can never escape from your Spirit!
   I can never get away from your presence!
If I go up to heaven, you are there;
   if I go down to the grave, you are there.
If I ride the wings of the morning,
   if I dwell by the farthest oceans,
even there your hand will guide me,
   and your strength will support me.
I could ask the darkness to hide me
   and the light around me to become night—
   but even in darkness I cannot hide from you.
To you the night shines as bright as day.
   Darkness and light are the same to you.
You made all the delicate, inner parts of my body
   and knit me together in my mother's womb.
Thank you for making me so wonderfully complex!
   Your workmanship is marvelous—how well I know it.
You watched me as I was being formed in utter seclusion,
   as I was woven together in the dark of the womb.
You saw me before I was born.
   Every day of my life was recorded in your book.
Every moment was laid out
   before a single day had passed.
How precious are your thoughts about me, O God.
   They cannot be numbered!
I can't even count them;
   they outnumber the grains of sand!
And when I wake up,
   you are still with me! (Psalm 139:1–18 NLT)

Remarkable! Take a moment to close your eyes and ponder the grandeur of our God. Next, take a moment to marvel at the fact that you are his masterpiece. You are not an accident or a mistake: you were created on purpose. God was not sleeping when he made you and he was not haphazardly putting pieces together. He watched over you in the womb, just as he watches over you every moment of every day. He was well aware of every intricate detail of your design. Yes, you and I are wonderfully complex beings, but God understands everything about us. You, my friend, are a miracle! You are marvelously created, and you possess gifts, talents, and experiences that are unique to you and only you. You were designed *on purpose* so that you could fulfill God's *purpose* for your life!

Marvel at Yourself

- Every human began as a single cell for about half an hour.
- The human heart beats about 40 million times a year.
- The aorta is the largest artery of the body; its diameter is about the same as a garden hose.
- The surface area of the lungs is about the same size as a tennis court.
- An average scalp has 100,000 hairs (and God know each one).
- It is impossible to tickle yourself. The cerebellum, a region in the posterior portion of your brain, warns the rest of your brain when you are attempting to tickle yourself.
- The brain is amazing! How much does the human brain think? 70,000 is the number of thoughts that it is estimated the human brain produces on an average day.

God is inconceivably bigger than you and your dreams. He is also omnipresent: there is no place in all creation where you can hide from his presence. That blows my mind! The Scriptures also tell us that God is omniscient: he perceives all things, and no fact can be hidden from his knowledge—not even the secrets of the heart (Psalm 44:21). Indeed, he understands our own intentions better than we do (Jeremiah 17:9–10; Hebrews 4:12 ESV). He knows about everything we have done and will do before we do it, yet graciously lays a blessing on your head and mine. As Paul explains, *"There is no creature hidden from His sight, but all things are naked and open to the eyes of Him to whom we must give account"* (Hebrews 4:13 NKJV).

Our God is omnipotent! He is all-ruling, he has all authority over all creation, and he reigns! That is why in him alone I feel a sense of security and why I trust his plans for me and for everyone and everything around me.

If God is present everywhere, all the time; knows all things; and is all-powerful, then I believe with all my heart that he has plans for us and we can trust that he knows, cares, and is able!

Now, take a moment to think about how God uniquely designed YOU to fulfill his dreams for your life.

What Is Your Picture of a Dream?

What comes to mind when you think of the word "dream"? A romantic relationship with your knight in shining armor? A daydream that takes your mind off your situation or a bad dream, causing worry and fear? A false hope or pie-in-the-sky, wild idea with no basis in reality?

If you are like me and enjoy sleeping, when you think of the word "dream," you may think of the series of thoughts and images that occur in your mind during the REM stage of sleep. Just as dreaming is a natural physiological function that is common to all of us and is necessary for maintaining adequate mental and emotional health, I believe having a dream, especially embracing God's dream for our lives, is necessary for maintaining thriving spiritual health. You may not have what you would consider big dreams, and that's just fine. Whether your dreams are big or small, they matter equally to God. One thing I want you to consider is that if God is a big God, who is able to do exceedingly, abundantly above and beyond what we can ever ask or imagine, why not dream big? (Ephesians 3:20). I'm just sayin', if God is the creator of the entire universe, owns everything, and is in complete and sovereign control, why not dream like it? Then let's do what we can do and God will do what we can't.

As I write this, it's mid-September and we are in the US 2012 presidential election season. If you live in the USA, the word "dream" may call one thing to mind: the American Dream. Incumbent President Barack Obama is ran for a second and final term. His major challenger was former Massachusetts governor, Republican Mitt Romney. All during the course of the election, we heard many speeches, promises, and warnings about this dream. The term "American Dream" is used in many ways, but it essentially suggests that anyone in the USA can succeed through hard work and has the potential to lead a happy, successful, and prosperous life. Because of the hardship we now find ourselves in, the pursuit and the decline of the American Dream have been the focus of the season and the focus of most Americans. Still, many have attained the American Dream while totally missing God's dream for their lives, so in reality they are living a nightmare.

John C. Maxwell defines a dream as "an inspiring picture of the future that energizes your mind, will, and emotions, empowering you to do everything you can to achieve it."[1] It's imperative to me that you know this is not a self-help book and it's not about "What the mind can believe, the will can conceive." Ecclesiastes 5:7 says, *"Talk is cheap, like daydreams and other useless activities. Fear God instead"* (NLT).

The focus of this book is holy dreaming and what God can do with a woman who loves and fears (reveres) him, who strives to seek him through a relationship, and who prays and obeys his divine will according to his word. When we seek him through prayer and his word, we are able to rely on his mighty energy to work within us and trust him to determine our steps.

Dreaming is a core part of who we are: *"It is God who works in you to will and to act in order to fulfill his good purpose"* (Philippians 2:13 NLT). True, not all of our dreams come from God, and not all of them are his will for our lives (more on that later), but the capacity to use our imaginations, to have visions, and to nurture desires is inherent in who he has created us to be, and *"he fulfills the desires of those who fear him"* (Psalm 145:19). Dreams and desires propel us forward. In many ways, they keep us moving toward heaven—they don't allow us to get too comfortable here, to settle in ways and places God never intended. As long as you are alive, God wants you to go further, dig deeper, and draw closer to him. I believe dreams are one of the primary ways he makes that happen.[2]

I confidently believe and have witnessed that God can work powerfully through any woman he chooses. Your age, race, circumstances, education level, and limitations *do not matter* if you will only surrender to him. No, my friend, it's never too late and you're not too messed up. God expects great things from us, but great things are composed of a lot of little things. Mother Teresa said, "Not all of us can do great things. But we can do small things with great love."

What Can Destroy, Derail, Detain, and Discourage Our Dreams?

> *Years may wrinkle the skin, but to give up enthusiasm wrinkles the soul.* —Douglas MacArthur

> *"The thief comes only to steal and kill and destroy; I have come that they may have life, and have it to the full."* (John 10:10)

I am sure many of us already know we have an enemy who plots and schemes to not only kill, steal, and destroy our dreams but our entire lives as well. The enemy comes to *kill* (slay, slaughter, take life) your dreams through the pain of a divorce or bad marriage, the permanent loss of a relationship, or the death of a loved one. Our maybe for you it's through health challenges or relational, financial, moral, or career disappointments. Many have been disappointed with God and church. The thief comes to steal (deceive, bamboozle, rob, take). Maybe someone told you to stop dreaming. They thought they were helping you by letting you know they didn't think you would ever accomplish that goal you set your heart on. He comes to destroy (fully demolish, obliterate, extinguish). One of the areas in life with which women struggle hardest is the hurt that family or children have caused. (More on that in Chapter Two.)

Above all, the thief comes to steal your identity. The day we moved into our first home in Atlanta, Georgia, as we drove into the subdivision, the weather was picture perfect, the neighborhood was inviting, and we were eager to finally get settled. As we approached our driveway, we saw a police car and a local TV station's van in front of our neighbor's house across the street. At that time, our neighborhood was known to have zero crime, so as you can imagine, we were apprehensive about all the activity. When we inquired about the situation, we were informed that the couple living in that house had just been arrested for identity theft. They were from another country and had taken on the identity of a different couple, so their whole life there had been a sham. They were serious criminals! I must confess, I had the heebie-jeebies for a little while just knowing that my husband, Mike, and I would have eventually met them and had them over for dinner to reach out to them. I know; I am from the Bronx, but I am ashamed to say I can still be a coward at times. I repented, prayed for them, and hoped for an opportunity to reach out to them, but we would never get to meet them because they were incarcerated for a substantial amount of time. Identity theft is serious and one of the fastest-growing crimes in the USA.[3]

As we look at the women of our society today, it seems that many of us are suffering with spiritual identity theft. Satan is the roaring lion and has an insatiable appetite for our souls. He has had girls and women on the top of his hit list from the beginning of time. He spots you and with hatred in him, he says, "There goes that dreamer!"

One of my favorite topics to discuss with women of all ages, races, and backgrounds is what their dreams are and what their plans are to achieve them. Those conversations have become the catalyst for this book.

As a Christian, do you have dreams for Christ, to be used to glorify him? If you do not profess to be a Christian, what are your dreams for your future, family, career, and life? To me, there is nothing like watching a woman light up with excitement as she begins to describe her dream, sometimes in vivid detail and with great passion.

My heart aches for the women who have never really had a dream because they can't grasp their valuable role as God's women. Also, at times, the demands of life keep us so busy just trying to get by that we feel like we do not have the time or oomph to dream. At other times, we tend to look at other people and assume that God must have a special dream or purpose for their lives, but not for ours. Many times we believe it's selfish for us to have our own dreams, whereas I believe sometimes it's selfish not to. Our dreams, when inspired by God, can change the world.

Here's the good news! I am so excited to proclaim a promise Jesus himself has made. He says, *"I have come that [you] may have life, and have it to the full."* Jesus has come to give us life that is richer and fuller on this earth and beyond measure because it's also eternal. He can give us back our dreams in an exceedingly abundant way!

I do not claim to be the "dream expert," nor do I claim to have all of the answers about how God works and will work in our lives—only God knows that! I am far from perfect, and I don't pretend to be a leadership guru. I am a normal disciple of Jesus who is fighting the good fight alongside my brothers and sisters. As I strive to live out my purpose as it is revealed in the Bible, God uncovers even bigger dreams for me than I could have ever imagined. In my experience, when I presume to know my purpose from my mind and not from the mouth of the Lord, I end up confused, frustrated, and unfulfilled. That is because God is intimately aware of the desires of our hearts, and I believe that in his masterful way he takes some of our desires and fulfills them within his purpose and dream for our lives.

It is illuminating to see women filled with hope when they realize that with God, everything is possible (Matthew 19:26). I visualize life returning to the body when a woman reclaims her dream and begins to imagine the possibilities. I feel a burden lifted when a woman realizes that she does not have to "fake" her dream, that she does not need permission to dream, and that she does not have to live someone else's dream.

And so I write…

I joyfully anticipate that on the pages of this book you will be inspired as you encounter and learn from both my biblical heroes and some of my "sheroes" in the faith today. Most likely, you will not recognize my sheroes' names or ever meet them personally, but as God's eyes range throughout the earth searching for those who will be faithful to him, I believe he takes note of them and strengthens their fully committed hearts (2 Chronicles 16:9). I pray that their personal and vulnerable sharing of faithfulness through the good, bad, and ugly times will enlighten you, stimulate you, and call you higher, and that you may see aspects of yourself and be reminded that you are not alone in your personal struggles, fears, and temptations.

At the end of each chapter, you will find a "Dream Dare" and a scripture for reflection. My hope is that you will challenge yourself to take the Dream Dare or make up your own for that chapter. Pray and ponder as you reflect on the scripture, and make a promise to put your Dream Dare into practice.

Finally, I pray to our Lord to open our eyes so we see wonderful things! I pray that his powerful word will give us confidence, conviction, and direction as we seek his will for our lives, and that as we pursue God and his dream for us, we will glean nuggets of his wisdom and understanding that will help direct us.

It is with humility, deep gratitude to God, and much respect for all of you that I write this book. I consider it an honor that you would go on this journey with me and I am excited to start traveling with you, my friend.

Together, let's dare to dream! It's our time!

_____ DREAM DARE _____

Dare to let God work in you to give you the desire and the power to please him.

For Reflection: pray...ponder...promise...practice.

For God is working in you, giving you the desire and the power to do what pleases him. (Philippians 2:13 NLT)

Chapter One

Daring to Dream Starts with Living on Purpose with Passon

God loves with a great love the man whose heart is bursting with a passion for the impossible. —William Booth

How blessed is God! And what a blessing he is! He's the Father of our Master, Jesus Christ, and takes us to the high places of blessing in him. Long before he laid down earth's foundations, he had us in mind, had settled on us as the focus of his love, to be made whole and holy by his love. Long, long ago he decided to adopt us into his family through Jesus Christ. (What pleasure he took in planning this!) He wanted us to enter into the celebration of his lavish gift-giving by the hand of his beloved Son. (Ephesians 1:3–6 MSG)

This scripture is mind-boggling! It is just breathtaking to know that God's love for me preceded the creation of the earth and goes on for eternity. God loved us and had us in mind. He created us to be like him, to be in his family, and to bring him glory and honor—not to be God, but to be godly, taking on his attitudes, values, and character. We were created for an eternal purpose far greater than any purpose for this life. You and I have a built-in instinct that leads us to long for a relationship with our heavenly Father—because *we were designed for that very thing!* Every one of us was made for the purpose of loving God and being with him for eternity (Matthew 22:37). His plan for us has always been to make us whole and holy. He loves us so much that he wants to give us every spiritual blessing in Christ (Ephesians 1:3), blessings like peace, joy, hope, and faith. He has an eternal dream for the estimated 3.5 billion women of the world today.

In everyone's life, there are those rare moments we hope never to forget. Some of the most precious and peaceful moments I remember from growing up are those when I got to sit alone on my front porch and look up to the sky asking God who he was, who I was supposed to be, and what I was supposed to do with my life. I reflected on deep questions like why he put me in the family I was in and what was my purpose on the earth. I knew God loved me, but how was he going to use this little girl from the Bronx to make a difference in this big world?

Somehow, deep in my heart, I believed even back then that God would answer my prayer and had a bigger purpose for me than I could ever imagine. I dreamed of serving the poor in Africa like Nobel Peace Prize winner Mother Teresa. I never wanted to be a nun because I always wanted a family, but I always dreamed of every child knowing that someone loves and cares for them.

What about you, beloved? Have you pondered your purpose in your heart? Have you come to realize what God's purpose is for you? To live with purpose means to strive toward a goal, to aim for a target, and to be intentional and resolute.

It is so satisfying to know that God himself does not want us to wander around aimlessly, not knowing why we are here. By his grace, he sent Jesus to ensure that every one of us would know that only in him can we find and fulfill our true purpose on this earth.

God Has Revealed Our Purpose in His Word

"From one man He has made every nationality to live over the whole earth and has determined their appointed times and the boundaries of where they live." (Acts 17:26 HCSB)

God loves us so much that he has worked out the geographical conditions necessary for creatures made in his image to reach out to him and find him. Therefore, we can devote ourselves to finding the truth, to reaching out to the Father.

Dear friends, let us love one another, for love comes from God. Everyone who loves has been born of God and knows God. Whoever does not love does not know God, because God is love. This is how God showed his love among us: He sent his one and only Son into the world that we might live through him.

This is love: not that we loved God, but that he loved us and sent his Son as an atoning sacrifice for our sins. Dear friends, since God so loved us, we also ought to love one another. No one has ever seen God; but if we love one another, God lives in us and his love is made complete in us. (1 John 4:7–12)

God's word is the nourishment for our soul that we all need. Through it, God illuminates the intentions and desires of his heart. He's not the big bad god in the sky pointing his finger at us every time we mess up. On the contrary, he sent his Son into the world so that we may live triumphantly, solely because he loves us.

Above all, it's all about that love! God doesn't settle for us being religious; he wants to have a real relationship with us. He wants us to love him back with all our hearts, not just say we love him. He implores us to love one another with all the love he has given us. Love is not an ushy-gushy feeling; the Bible shows in 1 Corinthians 13:4–7 that love is a decision. God's purpose is for us to choose to love him and love one another. In loving one another, several things happen: we get to know him better, we experience true life, and we are made complete in him. It is interesting to note that in the Bible, John says, *"God is love"* not *"love is God."* This is a very important point to remember, because sometimes when we women don't prioritize our love for God, we make love a god.

Love is one thing most women I know enjoy talking about. We like to share stories about who we are attracted to, or as married women, how we fell in love. Mike and I recently were reminiscing about when we blissfully fell in love.

In 1988 Michael Lorenzo Patterson moved from sunny Tallahassee, Florida to be a part of the New York City Church of Christ. He was chasing his dream of being trained in the ministry and eventually to go on a foreign mission team. God sent him to my neck of the woods, the Bronx, to join his dear friends Sam Powell and Frank Davis. His story is in his recently published book, *Running with Lions*. As he would tell it, when he first saw me in fellowship he thought I was gorgeous, so he avoided me because he wanted to remain focused on why he had moved to New York. By the way, when I saw him, I thought he was fine—my heart definitely skipped a beat.

Months after he made his home in one of the toughest neighborhoods in the south Bronx, he escorted me on our first date. I fondly remember our date in Westchester County, and since he picked me up from my home on the east side of the Bronx (as charming gentlemen do), we had an opportunity for a great car-ride conversation. I would venture to say he was enjoying the company and the conversation so much he almost crashed into another car on the highway, but thank God his angels were surrounding us as we were getting lost in each other's company. As we got to know each other, I was impressed by his love for God, his desire to do great things, and his learner's heart. It also helped that he was easy on the eyes and sounded like Luther Vandross (to me) when he sang. It didn't take me long to fall in love.

We dated for seven months then broke up for seven months and later got back together. During our time apart, we both grew tremendously in our own characters and eventually "he came crawling back to me." Yes, ladies, breakups in the kingdom are survivable (even if you stay in the same ministry). In fact, they can cause tremendous growth.

We women like to give love advice. Have you ever been advised that as a woman you need to find someone who loves you more than you love them? I have, and I am happy to say I found him. Mike's love for me gives me a glimpse of God's love for me, but in Christ I found the one who loved me first, sacrificially, unconditionally, perfectly, and eternally. We were created by his love (1 John 4:7–16), in his love, and for his pleasure. I know this sounds elementary, but imagine if every woman really believed it—if we all felt confident and secure in just this fact alone.

> *He has made everything beautiful in its time. He has also set eternity in the human heart; yet no one can fathom what God has done from beginning to end.* (Ecclesiastes 3:11)

At one time or another, every woman will feel an ache in her heart and an emptiness in her soul and will try to soothe it by filling it with something. Often, when we do not realize that it is God himself we are missing, we attempt to fill that emptiness with other people, money, careers, and countless other things, but *nothing else will fill that void.* Without a deep and meaningful relationship with God, at some point in our lives we will feel an emptiness that only he can fill. Our hearts are set on eternity, and our purpose centers around that astonishing fact.

> *In a large house there are things made out of gold and silver. But there are also things made out of wood and clay. Some have honorable purposes. Others do not. Suppose someone stays away from what is not honorable. Then the Master will be able to use him for honorable purposes. He will be made holy. He will be ready to do any good work.* (2 Timothy 2:20–21 NIrV)

God graciously desires to make us holy and to use us for his honorable purposes—how marvelous is that? That would be best for us, but *we must allow
him to use us as an instrument of his will.* Notice here that we have a choice to stay
away from sin and all of the things that would get in the way of what God
can do in our lives. Doing so allows us to be used by God, live with purpose,
and be made holy, ready for all the good work he has set out for us to accomplish. Just as gold, silver, wood, and clay are all different, God uses each of
us in different ways to fulfill his purposes. What are your godly personal or
kingdom dreams? How about your academic, financial, family, career, and
health dreams? Are they for God or for you to achieve goals and to acquire
wealth, prestige, favor, or power? Do you want to be a star, famous and
surrounded by admirers, or do you want to make God famous? One thing I
have learned is that it is not healthy to compare how God uses you with how
he uses someone else. You were designed on purpose so that you could fulfill
God's purpose for *your* life. Many times I wonder, "Why can't I sing like some
of the very talented young ladies in our ministry?" Well, God has made it
very clear that singing is not one of my talents that I can use for his purpose. I have known this for many years, but one of the more obvious ways
in which he made it clear was one Sunday when my friend Nia was sitting
next to me in church. As I sang my little heart out, she burst into exuberant
laughter. She was hysterically laughing about how my good friend Yolanda
and I were singing way off-key (and doing it loudly!). What can I say? I trust
her assessment—she is a professional singer and songwriter! We have to be
honest with ourselves and with each other. I take comfort in the fact that the
angels enjoy my singing and I accept the fact that my talents and my dreams
lie in other areas. Everything God created has purpose, and I was not created with that purpose in mind (if I were, you would get tired of hearing me!).

> *You guide me with your counsel,*
> *and afterward you will take me into glory.* (Psalm 73:24)

> *Where there is no vision [no redemptive revelation of God], the people
> perish; but he who keeps the law [of God, which includes that of man]—
> blessed (happy, fortunate, and enviable) is he.* (Proverbs 29:18 AMP)

Honestly, one of the (many!) mistakes I have made in the past has been
focusing too much on what someone else's vision for my life was. The Bible
does say that we must encourage one another and spur one another on toward love and good deeds (Hebrews 10:24). We do need relationships with

people who believe in us and are our biggest fans, and I hope everyone has these people, but God's dream for us must not solely depend on that! *You and I have got to become women who dare to dream whether we have many supporters or none.* There will be times when nobody else sees your vision. That is okay, because it is your vision. We must first seek God and be secure in the fact that he is our biggest fan. Your service should not depend upon praise and recognition from men, but only on making God smile and fulfilling his calling for your life that awaits you and you alone.

I am not saying that relationships are not important, and those who know me personally know that I believe the complete opposite. The Bible is full of "one another" scriptures because God created us to *need each other.* We need dear friends who know us, love us, and will tell us we can't sing if we really can't. Over the last twenty years, I have been fortunate to have women in my life who have genuinely loved me and believed that God could use me to live out his dream for my life to serve in and out of the full-time ministry. On top of that, they had the vision that I could grow, change, and learn to be a better disciple, wife, mother, and friend, and they were willing to help me get there. I am doubly blessed to have a husband who believes in me more than I believe in myself at times. His encouragement and advice propelled me into completing this book and into many other endeavors during our life together. As I write, my husband and I are serving in the full-time ministry at the Greater Atlanta Church of Christ, and I am surrounded and inspired by men and women who are pursuing their own dreams and challenging me never to stop pursuing mine. I need that!

> *We look at this Son and see the God who cannot be seen. We look at this Son and see God's original purpose in everything created. For everything, absolutely everything, above and below, visible and invisible, rank after rank after rank of angels—everything got started in him and finds its purpose in him.* (Colossians 1:15–16 MSG)

Everything and everyone finds their purpose in Christ. Only through him will you find *your* origin, *your* identity, *your* meaning, *your* significance, *your* destiny…*your dream.*

Once we capture or recapture God's purpose for our lives, then, and only then, can we begin to grab hold of his dream for us as it unfolds in our lives. Can you believe it? God desires to do things in you and through you that have never entered your mind and are beyond what you can imagine— things that are exceedingly beyond your wildest dreams!

Live with Passion

> Jesus Christ's life was an absolute failure from every standpoint but God's. But what seemed failure from man's standpoint was a tremendous triumph from God's, because God's purpose is never man's purpose. —Oswald Chambers, My Utmost for His Highest

What is passion? I would describe it as loving God wholeheartedly. If you want to know what passion looks like, look at Jesus. He did everything with passion. Look at everything God has created and accomplished. Why do you get up in the morning? What keeps you going? I'm not talking about hype or having zeal without knowledge (Proverbs 19:2); I'm talking about making the most we can out of the life we have. Without passion, life can be pretty mundane and predictable, but you and I are responsible for that. We can choose how we live. Are we brave or boring? Are we merely existing or are we exciting? Do we make our lives count or count the days till Friday? Are we courageous or cowards?

> Life should not be a journey to the grave with the intention of arriving safely in a pretty and well-preserved body, but rather to skid in broadside in a cloud of smoke, thoroughly used up, totally worn out, and loudly proclaiming "Wow! What a Ride!"[1]

We are on the greatest ride of our lives, so brace yourself: this is about a God thing!

Sometimes it feels like we're on a merry-go-round going in circles and sometimes like a rollercoaster speeding up and down hills with twists and turns. Sometimes it feels like we are in bumper cars blocked and bounced around, and sometimes on a slow-moving Ferris wheel, enjoying the moment and appreciating the beautiful sights. Whatever ride you happen to be on at this time in your life, don't forget to enjoy it. You won't be on it forever.

_____ DREAM DARE _____

Dare to discover who you really are and what you are living for.

For Reflection: pray...ponder...promise...practice.

It's in Christ that we find out who we are and what we are living for. Long before we first heard of Christ and got our hopes up, he had his eye on us, had designs on us for glorious living, part of the overall purpose he is working out in everything and everyone. (Ephesians 1:11–12 MSG)

Chapter Two

Jesus Loves Me, This I Know

[God's] love for us was displayed most clearly through the cross of Christ. There our Lord stretched out His bloodstained hands to say, "I love you this much!" —Dillon Burroughs[1]

> *I am your Creator.*
> *You were in my care*
>   *even before you were born.*
> *Israel, don't be terrified!*
> *You are my chosen servant,*
>   *my very favorite.* (Isaiah 44:2 CEV)

As I reflect on my early years, the first thoughts I have are of the poetry and lullabies my mom often wrote and tenderly sang to my brother, Jay, and me as she tucked us into bed. "Just close your eyes and dream away; tomorrow is another day, my sweet, so tiny and sweet." Mom probably had no idea how those lullabies made me feel what God had declared long ago: that he cherished me before I was born and that I am his very favorite. Those lullabies are enshrined in my memory, and those demulcent lullaby moments are some of the sweetest memories of my childhood.

Zephaniah 3:17 says,

> *The LORD your God is with you,*
>   *the Mighty Warrior who saves.*
> *He will take great delight in you;*
>   *in his love he will no longer rebuke you,*
>   *but will rejoice over you with singing.*

Evidently, God used my mom to rejoice over me with singing. In fact, I believe God used those times to plant seeds of his unfailing, unconditional love for me that would tuck me in for a lifetime. Since I was a little girl, deep down in my heart I have always been sure of God's presence in my life and secure in his personal and unconditional love for me. Of course, I take no credit for that. Mom (who was not a super-religious woman) taught me that God not only lavished me with love (1 John 3:1), but adored me and had his angels vigilantly surrounding me to protect me. She always expressed that God had a great plan for my life. I can say I am eternally grateful that in those early years God used Mom to nourish and plant the seeds of love deep in my heart that would take root and one day grow into an everlasting love for God and others. Mom was a supermom in the very early years. I do think that being present for your children (especially from birth through age five) and planting seeds of love in their hearts is one of the most enriching gifts you can give them.

My prayer and deep desire is for every little girl on the planet to know God's incomparable love for her. He rejoices over them with singing and is a mighty warrior who fights for them. Anybody who knows me knows I love little children and that I have a special place in my heart for God's little princesses. As much as we all love children, that could never equate to the love and compassion God has for them. He says in Psalm 127:3 (NASB) that children are a gift from him, and I believe God sees little girls as good and perfect gifts from heaven (James 1:17). The Bible warns against ignoring, despising, or mistreating them. God is indignant about anyone hindering them, and, to be sure, anyone who hurts children will be punished (Matthew 18:6). Don't mess with the children!

Understanding who we really are at the core of our being starts with knowing whose we are. Fortunately, Genesis 1 and 2 answer the fundamental questions that most women have or will consider: what is my origin, my identity? Who am I really? In Genesis 2 we find that we are a special creation of God, made in his image and likeness, and meant to enjoy fellowship with him.

God's Love Story from the Beginning of Mankind

Adam, the first man, gives us an example of how God created us. God formed Adam from the dust of the ground and breathed into his nostrils the breath of life (Genesis 2:7). Can you just imagine this? Now that's what you call awesome! Then God placed Adam in the Garden to work it and take care of it (Genesis 2:15). Adam was a complete being, enjoying his fellowship with God, but something was missing. He was alone because before Eve there was no one to love. God told him, in effect, "You have the animals, but they aren't like you." Animals were created for man's enjoyment and although they can give us comfort, they cannot fulfill a person's need for love.[2]

Eve, the first woman and wife and the mother of all living, was created as part of God's great dream for humankind. She was God's great idea and the amazing finale of his creation. Eve was designed out of love, God's grace, and the deep desire for the perfect companion and soul mate to stand alongside man. It always makes me smile when I think of how God made the woman. God put Adam to sleep and, while Adam rested, took a rib from him. Working his great wonders, from that rib God shaped Eve. The Hebrew expression describing how God "made" (the rib) into a women denotes careful construction and design. Literally, it means God built a woman. Sensational! I just feel a special honor and privilege to be a woman distinctly designed by my Creator with tender loving care and in such a special manner. Building the woman was totally God's grace to humankind. Eve came from God and shared man's exact substance. She was not less valuable, not an afterthought, and not less loved. She was a great gift to the world, she was fashioned perfectly so that man and woman would complement each other, and she was beautiful in God's eyes. The Bible does not give us a description of Eve's appearance but it does record that Adam broke out into poetry and song when he saw her (Genesis 2:23).[3]

So what happened? The man and woman strolled naked and unashamed in Paradise. Can you imagine: uninterrupted fellowship with God, no fear, no hatred, no problems, and no drama? Then one day, Satan, that old devil, came into the picture disguised as a crafty serpent. As we continue on to Genesis 3, we quickly find that God has an adversary who in his pride and rebellion wanted to and still wants to be above God (Revelation 12:7–10) and has an unending hatred of God and his creation (1 Peter 5:8). His evil plan was to tempt Eve to disobey God. She succumbed to temptation, Adam agreed, and they both ate the fruit of the tree. They rejected God's plan and pursued their own desires. Adam and Eve's deliberate rebellion against God ultimately led to broken fellowship with God and the fall of humanity.[4]

Prior to reading the Bible for myself, I was inherently aware that some things I was doing were sin, but I did not have an understanding of what sin really was and how it hurts me, those around me, and God. To sin is to rebel against God and against his divine will, rejecting his love, authority, and wisdom. Satan uses the same tricks on us today that he used then.

Holley Gerth, in her book, *You're Made for a God-Sized Dream*, describes Satan's modus operandi: "Ever since Eden, the enemy has come at us with a million different versions of the same question, 'Did God really say…?' And many times those questions are aimed squarely at our dreams. Did God really say you have what it takes? Did God really say that's what you're supposed to do? When you follow your God-sized dreams, you'll face many external obstacles. But the biggest threats are from the inside."[5]

I can totally relate to giving in to those temptations. Even though I love God with all my heart, at times when my relationship with him is not close, I too start listening to Satan's lies, questioning my contentment, and becoming ungrateful, and, doubting God's goodness and provision, I begin to rebel against him and his word. In my pride, I can start thinking that my way may be better than God's way. I'm sure we can all relate, because no temptation has overtaken us except what is common to mankind (1 Corinthians 10:13). Eve is typical of us all.

Tragically, Adam and Eve's choice to disobey God, trade the truth for a lie, and fall from God's gracious presence affected all creation to this day. They chose pride over Paradise, and when sin entered the world, man started departing from God's original plan and purpose and damaged the image God originally had for us.

Thankfully, the story does not end here. There is good news! In the midst of Adam and Eve's sin, we witness God's grace. God made Eve a promise that her seed would crush the serpent's head and her own offspring would destroy the destroyer.[6] Ultimately, Satan did not win the battle for men's souls; Jesus won the war on that old rugged cross. He is our redeemer and the living, breathing example of whom God wants us to be like and how he wants us to live.

That is the good news I pray every woman and every precious little girl on God's earth will know. I implore you that as you look at Eve, be amazed at our own original design and God's desire and purpose for us to be like him and have the ability to share many of his characteristics. I feel so honored to share in his emotions, values, appreciation of beauty, creativity, power, and sacrifice for others, which all reflect his glory. My security comes from knowing I am his, and my identity is found in the God who made us. We don't have to wander aimlessly and hopelessly trying to find ourselves.

To illustrate this point, I think of the Lifetime movie *Abducted: The Carlina White Story*. The movie was based on the true story of a girl who was abducted from a New York hospital as an infant and was reunited with her birth parents after twenty-three years. It was the visual aid for how miserable it is to be lost, not know who you are or where you come from, and end up living someone else's deluded reality. It was so sad I cried my heart out for Carlina and for the countless other children who are still missing in this world.

Spiritually, that doesn't have to be us, dear friends. We are all God's children and we don't have to figure out our identity on our own or through what others think of us. We don't have to let men, media, or money define us. We can know who we are, whose we are, and where we belong. We share fully in man's identity, making us no less valuable, not an afterthought, and no less loved. We are God's great gift to the world, and every one of us is beautiful in God's eyes and extravagantly loved.

I am equally beholden to God for his glorious creation of the male, and I am indebted to the godly men that he has put in my life and for the role and responsibility that God has given them. He has designed and equipped men and women differently for various tasks in such a superb way that we would need each other to bring honor to him.

Jesus Loves the Little Children

Many of us had our dreams as little girls. We wanted to become mothers, teachers, businesswomen, doctors, or lawyers. My dear friend Cristelle once shared with me that her dream as a little girl was to be president of her country, the Dominican Republic. If you were anything like me, you dressed up and role-played and even talked to yourself as you pretended to be the person of your dreams.

For some of us, that scenario never entered our minds. Maybe our childhood was more of a nightmare stolen by our abuser or the person who neglected us. As a child of alcoholics, I can relate to having to dig through the rubble left from the destruction of alcoholism. Many of us have been scared, hurt, and healing or needing to heal from the pain that the folks closest to us inflicted. We find ourselves not able to dream with a God who loves, because we are still dealing with those who did not love us. I'm also thinking of the many women who have been worn down by unhealthy relationships, sexual abuse, mental and physical illness, and tragedy and feel as though any dream they may have had has been incinerated by the fires of a hell on earth.

No matter what has happened in your past or what is happening presently, you are never to be forgotten by God. His fatherly love can more than conquer our past, heal every wound, mend us where we are broken, take care of all our needs, and secure our future. His love affectionately draws us close to his heart, gently leading and guiding us, and carrying us when we need it.

God Loves Us like a Father

> *He tends his flock like a shepherd:*
> > *He gathers the lambs in his arms*
> *and carries them close to his heart;*
> > *he gently leads those that have young.* (Isaiah 40:11)

"*He is a father to the fatherless, a defender of widows*" (Psalm 68:5). God says he will not forget us, he has inscribed us on the palm of his hand, and our walls are ever before him. Even if our human mothers and fathers failed to love and nurture us, the Lord could never fail to love us (Isaiah 49:15–16). He welcomes children and is their home and sanctuary. He is the one who lifts your head high (Psalm 3:3). Your Daddy wants to gather you in his arms, carry you close to his heart, and gently lead you home. One of my personal favorite scriptures is Deuteronomy 32:10–11:

> *In a desert land he found him,*
> > *in a barren and howling waste.*
> *He shielded him and cared for him;*
> > *he guarded him as the apple of his eye,*
> *like an eagle that stirs up its nest*
> > *and hovers over its young,*
> *that spreads its wings to catch them*
> > *and carries them aloft.*

God Loves Us like a Mother

Take a moment to feel the motherly and fatherly love of God as he wraps his arms around us. In God's word, images of both mother and father are used to depict his relationship with us. In Isaiah 66:13 God says that he is like a mother who comforts her child. In Isaiah 49:15 he says,

> "*Can a mother forget the baby at her breast*
> > *and have no compassion on the child she has borne?*
> *Though she may forget,*
> > *I will not forget you!*"

We all have a testimony. We may not all feel inclined to write a book about it, but I believe we should all be telling our story. Being active in sharing our faith, we will grow in our understanding of every good thing we have in Christ and be a light to a dark world (Philemon 6). I share part of my story below and throughout this book as a testimony to how much God was always right there loving me even when I didn't feel it, and how he has worked in all things for my good to ultimately fulfill his dream for my life. He's masterfully working in me and he's working in you.

Jesus Loves Me in the Good Times

> *God wasn't attracted to you and didn't choose you because you were big and important—the fact is, there was almost nothing to you. He did it out of sheer love, keeping the promise he made to your ancestors. God stepped in and mightily bought you back out of that world of slavery, freed you from the iron grip of Pharaoh king of Egypt. Know this: God, your God, is God indeed, a God you can depend upon. He keeps his covenant of loyal love with those who love him and observe his commandments for a thousand generations.* (Deuteronomy 7:7–9 MSG)

Much later in life I would discover that my mom (affectionately known as Mama BJ to all the neighborhood kids) was a musical genius who learned to play classical piano at three years old. Yes, I said three. Although Mama BJ was legally blind, deaf in one ear, and partially deaf in the other, she learned to play the piano by ear and sing angelically.

Moreover, if you had met my mom back then, you would have thought she was charming, lighthearted, sweet, energetic, and a giving woman who was crazy about her man, Joe. As a little girl, I noticed that dad was crazy about mom too. My dad, affectionately known as "Uncle Joe" or "Papa Joe," was the seventh of ten children of Armitine Whiting and McKinley Reid. Dad served in the Air Force from 1953 to 1957 and was very proud to be an Air Force man. He was a handsome and hardworking man who worked for the New York City Housing Authority as a foreman for twenty-five years and was very proud to have a city job. Growing up, I can't recall him ever missing a day of work (later on you will see why that was significant). He was an avid sports fan (Mets, Nicks, and boxing), and I think we all got our love of sports from him (I am a diehard Nicks and Yankees fan). They were married thirty-five years before he passed.

My fondest memories of my relationship with my dad are from when

I was a teenager. He and I would practice pitching in front of our house and he would give me tips on my fastball. He was so proud that his little girl had a passion for the same game he had enjoyed and played all his life.

Our individual childhood experiences vary from person to person. There is not a perfect family, but there are families that are more healthy, functional, loving, and nurturing than others. If you grew up in that atmosphere, you may have primarily pleasant memories. If you grew up on the opposite side of that spectrum in a dysfunctional family, you may have very few pleasant memories or you may not have any at all. If you are like me, your childhood was a combination of both happy times and hard times.

In my elementary school years, many of my good times happened right on 228th street. It was a privilege to grow up on a block that in the '70s was a great and safe neighborhood in the East Bronx. I grew up with about fifteen to twenty kids all around the same age. If you have ever seen the movie *Crooklyn*, you've seen my neighborhood with its mixture of races and cultures. All the kids were good friends but not without the normal amount of drama.

Summers were and still are my favorite time of the year. The days were spent with my girlfriends either at the pool, swimming and sunbathing (I enjoyed drinking in the sun's warmth), or practicing softball. I immensely loved the ocean and still do. Sitting along the shore looking out at God's magnificent creation is my favorite place to be to this day. Whenever I need a spiritual revival and to be reminded of the grandeur of God, I get to the nearest ocean or I close my eyes and picture one.

After dark, we gathered on someone's porch, telling stories and playing Chinese School and card games like Spades, 500, and Old Maid. We also contrived ways to raise money for our trips and so on, so we planned variety shows that we would perform to raise funds. Even though we lived on a busy one-way street, we played Ringolario, tag, softball, Red Light/Green Light, Simon Says, and Run Catch and Kiss. Our parents would not have been pleased about that last one.

Hands down, playing softball with my girlfriends, Yvette, Deidre, Sylvia, Carmen, and Jackie, was the best activity in the neighborhood. We played softball for two leagues, and that kept us on the go. I am so thankful for our coach—I'll call him Mr. O—and for Mrs. Souto (Sylvia, Carmen, and Maria's mom), who chaperoned us on most of our trips. They kept us out of a lot of the trouble kids get into when they are bored. One of my best-loved movies is *A League of Their Own*, a 1992 American comedy-drama. It tells a fictionalized account of the real-life All-American Girls Professional

Baseball League and stars Geena Davis, Lori Petty, Tom Hanks, Madonna, and Rosie O'Donnell.[7] Jimmy Dugan (played by Tom Hanks), the coach for the Rockford Peaches, reminds me of Mr. O., who made us practice against the men's teams in Edenwald projects. They were tough and it was intimidating to play against them, but Mr. O made them play against us as if they were playing men. I imagine he would have said just what Jimmy Dugan said to one of his players when she started crying because he said something rude: "Are you crying? Are you crying? Are you crying? There's no crying! There's NO CRYING IN BASEBALL!" Another favorite line of mine is when Dottie (the star player) is thinking about quitting because she said, "It just got too hard," and Jimmy Dugan's response is, "It's supposed to be hard. If it wasn't hard, everyone would do it. The hard...is what makes it great." I think that was Mr. O's mindset also and as a result, one year we won the state championship. Wow, what a priceless experience. We learned discipline by practicing and working hard every day, we learned teamwork, we tasted victory, and we tasted defeat. Mr. O and Mrs. Souto have passed on, but their memory will live with me forever.

Summer vacations were indelible as well. My dad had eleven siblings, so I had a wonderful time getting to know them and my cousins. Either they were visiting us or I was spending time on Long Island at Aunt June's house with some of my precious cousins, Cindy, Star, Adam, Jay, Trinetta, Bebe, and Shaun. For a city girl that was a great treat. I am particularly indebted to Aunt June, Uncle Donald, and Uncle Conrad for the role they played in my life. I always say between those two uncles and my dad I had one fantastic father.

Aquinas High School was a place of refuge for me. My family would have been considered upper-lower class on the socioeconomic scale and really could not afford to send my brother and me to private school, but my mom sacrificed her Social Security disability check and babysitting money to do so. Mama BJ babysat and basically helped raise a lot of the kids in our neighborhood, charging their parents a miniscule amount because she had compassion on them and their situations. No matter what state of mind she was in, her heart was very sacrificial in so many ways.

When I was a teenager I didn't appreciate at the time the things my parents did for me, like the way they sacrificed to send me to the schools I attended and provide the good teachers I was blessed with. In April 2012 I attended my thirtieth-year high school reunion and was filled with a gratitude I had never really felt before. As I walked through the halls of my alma mater, I was overwhelmed with the realization that Aquinas was yet another way that God had been working in the details of my life to fulfill his dream for me.

Aquinas, an all-girls' Catholic high school, is located in the South Bronx. The neighborhood around the school has progressed now, but back in those days it was rough. Outside Aquinas's walls was frightening to me, but inside was a beautiful, bright, immaculately kept school with teachers who were truly fond of me and friends who are like sisters to this day. It was the perfect atmosphere for learning, and it helped to prepare me for life. I enjoyed school, was a cheerleader, played softball and basketball, and even became student council president in my senior year. God had begun teaching me that even though I had my own problems at home I could still serve and care about other people. My fellow Aquinites and I used to sing, "A.Q.U.I.N.A.S., Aquinas, the best" and to this day I am convinced it was.

Those were some of the good times that stand out in my memory, and as I look back now, I can see how God was working his wonders by using those times along with the bad times to draw me closer and closer to his plan and dream for my life.

Surely your goodness and unfailing love will pursue me
all the days of my life,
and I will live in the house of the LORD
forever. (Psalm 23:6 NLT)

God really wants us to understand his desire for each and every one of us. "The word 'pursue' means: to search for eagerly, to track down, to hunt for someone with relentless abandon, to chase, to pursue ardently and to run after. It is to relentlessly pursue and chase after someone until you hunt them down."[8]

What comes to my mind is the movie *Taken*, starring Liam Neeson as Bryan Mills. The movie is about seventeen-year-old Kim, the daughter of Mills, a retired agent who leaves the Central Intelligence Agency and moves to be near Kim and her mother in California. As typical teens do when they really want something, Kim convinces Mom and Dad to let her travel to Paris with a friend. Not long after arriving in Paris, an Albanian gang of human traffickers kidnaps the girls. Kim courageously sneaks a call to her dad to alert him of her kidnapping, and he immediately takes off in hot pursuit to search for his daughter and her friend and to kill the kidnappers. That father had an intensity, urgency, and passion to chase down the villains. He made a wholehearted effort with extraordinary energy and deep conviction.[9]

When I think of God's goodness and unfailing love pursuing me, it takes my breath away that God is tracking me down just to be good to me and show me how much he loves me. "The word translated 'unfailing love' is the Hebrew word chesed, which is so full of meaning that no single English word can capture it. This Hebrew word simply has no equivalent in the English language... *The New Strong's Expanded Dictionary of Bible Words* states there are three basic meanings to the word which always interact, and they are 'strength,' 'steadfastness,' and 'love.' The essence of the word is a robust love that never fades or falters; this love is completely reliable and constant."[10] It's a total commitment of God to us as his children unconditionally, completely, and eternally. That kind of love sweeps me off my feet.

_____ DREAM DARE _____

Dare to be open to how God can use the good times and the bad times in your life, to accomplish his dream for you.

For Reflection: pray...ponder...promise...practice.

> *When times are good, be happy;*
> *but when times are bad, consider this:*
> *God has made the one*
> *as well as the other.* (Ecclesiastes 7:14a)

Chapter Three

He Loved Me in My Slimy Pit

The only genuine love worthy of the name is unconditional.
—John Powell

> *He lifted me out of the slimy pit,*
> *out of the mud and mire.* (Psalm 40:2a)

> *Long ago the LORD said to Israel:*
> *"I have loved you, my people, with an everlasting love.*
> *With unfailing love I have drawn you to myself."*
> (Jeremiah 31:3 NLT)

As a result of the fall, this world is profoundly broken. No matter how wonderful an individual or family may be, we are all affected by sin's curse and are incapable of being perfectly in tune with the ideal of Eden.[1] As John 16:33 says, *"In this world you will have trouble. But take heart! I have overcome the world."*

At this time, I have to make a confession. As I begin to divulge some of our family secrets and expose some of the skeletons in our family closet, I feel tempted with guilt about "airing my family's dirty laundry." We were raised that way, especially in the African American community. We were taught, "What happens in this house stays in this house." Even now, I feel tempted with the thought that I would be betraying my parents (who both became Christians and went on to Paradise, Amen) or embarrassing my relatives by telling the truth about our home. That is primarily the reason

I never told anybody what was really going on at home until I became a Christian at age twenty.

I have learned that God is light (1 John 1:5) and he does not want anyone to live in darkness, rather he exposes the deeds of the darkness so that we can be free. It is with that heart and spirit that I share with you our "dirty laundry" and pray that if there is one person out there who will be emboldened to hold onto her dreams even through dark times, it will be worth it.

Most certainly, both Mom and Dad were wonderful people who had their own demons and consistently consumed alcohol as far back as I can remember. Dad was an alcoholic since he was a teen and Mom started with a few beers after Dad got off work then rapidly progressed to full-blown addiction. This made life inside the walls of 1017 East 228th Street very unpredictable, stressful, terrifying, and at times perilous. That's why I loved sitting on my front porch.

During this time in my life, there were no more lullabies at bedtime. Instead, bedtime was when the nightmare began for my brother and me. Some nights were easier than others. The easy nights were those when I stayed awake to make sure the cigarettes were put out and my parents were put to bed. My brother was always willing to help, but I usually persuaded him to go to sleep so he could be ready for school the next day. No sense in us both being stressed out and tired the next morning. Unfortunately, for many years our parents got drunk almost daily.

The dreadful nights were the nights the arguing escalated into physical altercations and my brother and I would run downstairs to physically restrain our parents because we feared they would hurt each other. Hiding things seemed to become the norm for Jay and me. We hid knives, car keys (so they would not venture out to the 24-hour liquor store around the corner), and liquor bottles, and we absolutely hid the truth from everyone outside our walls.

Later in life, I would learn that Dad was defined as a functioning alcoholic. He was sort of cantankerous, tough as nails, and a man of few words, but after a few drinks he was expressive, amiable, and hilariously funny. As horrible as this may sound, we actually liked him better drunk.

On the other hand, when Mom was sober she was very sweet. I knew she loved me fiercely and she was so good at making me feel every bit of her love. After a night of drinking, her behavior would change for the worse, and the next morning she could hardly function. I nursed her hangovers before going to school and lied to the neighbors when they asked what was going on the night before because they had heard all the fuss. The very frustrating thing was that the next day, my parents would never remember what had happened when they got drunk the night before.

In the old days, we were fortunate enough to own two black-and-white TVs that had four to five channels. (For the younger generation, that's a TV that plays only in black and white—no colors). We had no cable. My family enjoyed watching our favorite TV shows, which were *I Love Lucy*, *The Brady Bunch*, *The Partridge Family*, *Sanford and Son*, and *The Jeffersons*. I remember thinking, "Why is my family not like them?" And that made me angry. I started to feel and verbalize my anger about the situation. Why couldn't I have a normal family? Why did my parents let a liquid in a bottle ruin their lives and ours? I blamed my dad for it all and despised him. I knew God loved me, but I could not understand why he wouldn't step in, help us, and save us—just make them stop.

Living in that level of dysfunction, I carried inside of me a constant fear that somebody would get hurt at home or that my parents would divorce. I was afraid of what people thought about my parents, and every evening I was afraid to come home and bring my friends with me, because I didn't know what condition everybody would be in. I later learned that that worry and fear were the cause of my constant headaches and stomachaches. What concerned me most was the possibility of divorce. Even the thought of that was gut wrenching. I thought, "I love them both so much; who would I live with? Oh, my God, if that happens, my family would be more messed up than it is now." Like many of you, I cried myself to sleep many nights. I am now comforted to know that God kept track of all my sorrows and collected all my tears in his bottle. He recorded each one in his book. He cares!

In all their distress he too was distressed,
and the angel of his presence saved them.
In his love and mercy he redeemed them;
he lifted them up and carried them
all the days of old. (Isaiah 63:9)

When I reminisce about my teen years, I have the utmost appreciation for many of the blessings I have previously mentioned, and I am especially thankful to have survived through that very tumultuous season (and I'm not being dramatic).

With every teen birthday, I willingly descended farther into the slimy pit of rebellion, deceit, hatred, anger, selfishness, fear, and lust. By this time, I was searching for love in all the wrong places. I mastered the art of looking good on the outside, and I was the consummate people pleaser. To the world, I looked like I had it together, always wore a big smile, and was nicknamed Sunshine by one of my teachers.

Although I had seen what the use and abuse of alcohol had done to my family, I did not have a conviction that I needed to stay away from drugs and alcohol. As a teen, I started smoking cigarettes and marijuana, drinking alcohol (thank God I did not like the taste), and sniffing cocaine. The weed made me feel out of control so I hated it, and the cocaine gave me a headache (Amen). It is only by the grace of God that I did not become an addict, because I have a genetic disposition due to the prevalence of alcoholism in my family.

Like many inner-city kids, going away to college was and is our ticket out of the ghetto. For me, it meant getting away from all the dysfunction at home. It had not occurred to me that I was leaving the dysfunction at home and going into the dysfunctional world. Thank you, God, for providing me with a best friend named Ben who was my confidant and bodyguard. He took me under his wing and helped me navigate my first year at Boston College.

Moving to Boston, Massachusetts was a culture shock to me. In the '80s Boston was still a very racially prejudiced town, and I was ill equipped to handle the discrimination. The student population at Boston College was pretty much all Caucasian; and remember, I'm the girl from the Bronx. I grew up with and went to school with a very diverse population, and to some extent, I thought racism was a thing of the past until I arrived at Boston College. For days, I'd walk on campus and never see a person of color. During my time on Chestnut Hill, the worst kind of prejudice I experienced was not being called the derogatory "N" word or having rocks thrown at me as I walked at night to the dorms (yes, that actually happened). It was the experience of being invisible, being ignored. Ben and I used to sit at the counter at the pop (soda) shop, and the waiter would choose to serve everyone around us and ignore us. In class, I would raise my hand to answer the professor's question and he would somehow never see my hand. On line in the cafeteria, students just got in front of me as if I were not even there. I had never remembered feeling prejudice before, but when I experienced it, I hated it.

I believe God sent me to Boston College for a few reasons. It was an amazing educational experience that I am grateful to have had, and it was also where I met one of the most courageous women I know, Sandy Ripley O'Toole. On our first day, I arrived at the dorms excited to meet my new roommate. When Sandy and her family walked in the door, it was a great surprise for both of us. She's part Irish and German, with dirty blonde hair and a weird accent (no offense, Bostonians). I would later find out that Sandy was from Avon, Massachusetts, a town with an African-American population back then of zero. In fact, I was the first African-American with whom she and her family had interacted. She had only seen us on TV and when she drove into Boston to go to the bus station. Again, I was given a gift from God in Sandy's family. It was as if God was showing me that not everyone was going to be like those "rock throwers." Sandy's down-to-earth family loved me from the start and was welcoming and kind to me. God knew I needed Sandy and the home away from home that her family provided, and he knew she needed me.

Our first day was memorable because we had a few communication bloopers. For example, she asked me if I like to potty (party) and if I pock (park) the cah (car). We made it through our communication problems by agreeing that the other spoke funny, but there was one thing I didn't think we'd survive, and that was each other's music. Sandy loved rock (hard rock) and I was the disco queen. Disco made her physically ill (I'm not joking) and I hated rock with a passion. We learned to compromise, and somehow we made it through and became best friends. In fact, after the first semester, most of the people on our dorm floor switched roommates to be with whom they were most comfortable, and we were probably the only ones that did not. By this time, our hearts were knit together. I'm so proud of us, Sandy!

Throughout that year, I had the pleasure of visiting her home and spending time with her family (whom I thought were like the Cleavers), and she came home with me to New York City over the Christmas break. I love my Sandy, but she almost got us killed in the Bronx on the Number 2 train. She was intrigued by the graffiti on the inside of the train, took out her camera, and started taking pictures. The people on the train started squirming and covering their faces because they thought she was taking pictures of them. In case you didn't know, taking pictures of people you don't know can be dangerous in New York. We laughed so hard about that and all of Sandy's adventures there.

That was the Christmas I took out a $3000 loan to buy my mom a very special gift, a fine china and silverware set. Good intentions, bad idea. I was a poor college student! Long story short, one of my extended family members (who was an alcoholic and living with us at the time) took the set around the corner to our favorite delicatessen called Eddie's (today it would be called a bodega) and sold it for $40 to buy alcohol. As you can imagine,

I was angrier than words can describe. I felt hopeless about ever having a "normal" family, and I was so embarrassed.

The following year, Sandy's family went through one of the most painful crises a family can go through. Honestly, I was shocked that her family had problems. I know that sounds naïve, but up to that point I really did think most people outside my world had perfect families. But that was far from the truth. I love Sandy so much and am so glad she confided in me and that I was able to be there during that time in her life. She amazed me with her discipline to stay focused in her studies as she persevered through an emotionally challenging time.

The next year, Sandy was diagnosed with cancer. In typical "Sandy style," she inspired everyone with the way she bravely faced her cancer treatments, not missing a beat in school and triumphantly graduating on time and cancer-free.

My first year of college was also the time in my life when I began to feel emptiness and a need for God because of the sin in my life and not because of my parents' issues. God knew my heart was opening up, and he sent a campus sister from the Boston Church of Christ to reach out to me. I am ashamed to say that instead of accepting the invitation to learn more about Jesus, I thought I knew more than she did (I apologize, Sherry Barlow) and did not pursue the opportunity to know God at that time. I needed more humbling.

Out of the Mud

I will never forget my second semester at Boston College. Instead of seriously pursuing God or my education, I pursued relationships with men to try to fill the emptiness in my heart and make me happy. I compromised what few standards I did have, and as a result, I ended up in several bad relationships. Consequently, I underwent one of the worst experiences in my life, a date-rape situation.

The date rape actually happened before I had ever heard it referred to as "date rape," and it was devastating. Rape is both physically and emotionally horrifying, and when someone you know rapes you, it can also be extremely confusing.

When people think of rape, they might think of a stranger jumping out of a shadowy place and sexually attacking someone. But it's not only strangers who rape. In fact, about half of all people who are raped know the person who attacked them. Girls and women are most often raped, but guys also can be raped.

Most friendships, acquaintances, and dates never lead to violence, of course. But, sadly, sometimes it happens. When forced sex occurs between two people who already know each other, it is known as date rape or acquaintance rape.

Even if the two people know each other well, no one has the right to force a sexual act on another person against his or her will.

Although it involves forced sex, rape is not about sex or passion. Rape has nothing to do with love. Rape is an act of aggression and violence.

You may hear some people say that those who have been raped were somehow "asking for it" because of the clothes they wore or the way they acted. That's wrong: The person who is raped is not to blame. Rape is always the fault of the rapist. And that's also the case when two people are dating—or even in an intimate relationship. One person never owes the other person sex. If sex is forced against someone's will, that's rape.

Alcohol is often involved in date rapes. Drinking can loosen inhibitions, dull common sense, and—for some people—allow aggressive tendencies to surface.

Drugs may also play a role. You may have heard about "date-rape" drugs like rohypnol ("roofies"), gamma-hydroxybutyrate (GHB), and ketamine. Drugs like these can easily be mixed in drinks to make a person black out and forget things that happen. Both girls and guys who have been given these drugs report feeling paralyzed, having blurred vision, and lack of memory.

Always order your own drinks and watch them being made. Drugs can be slipped into both alcoholic and nonalcoholic drinks at parties or in bars without a person knowing. And don't drink from your glass if it has been left where you can't keep an eye on it.

Mixing these drugs with alcohol is highly dangerous and can kill.[2]

Rape is a violent crime, and I should have reported it, but because the attacker was an acquaintance and I willingly went to his dorm room (under false pretenses), I doubted whether it was rape and didn't think anyone would even believe my story.

For months after the rape, I felt a range of emotions and kept everything inside. I had to continue to see the guy who raped me because he worked in the cafeteria, and when we saw each other, he acted as if he never knew me. I was disgusted by him and distressed at the thought of all the girls to whom he must have done this. He seemed to have a routine. I stopped trusting some of the girls I considered friends (not Sandy), because one night when I was lying in bed in my dorm, I overheard them in the hallway gossiping about my situation, saying that I really wanted it to happen. I was devastated and so disappointed by their betrayal of trust. Since becoming a Christian, I have forgiven the rapist and left him in God's hands, and I have forgiven the girlfriends from my heart, so girls, if you are reading this, I want you to know I love you. I do regret being a coward at that time and not reporting the rape to save other girls.

Satan is on the rampage seeking someone to devour (1 Peter 5:8). Peer pressure as well as questions and confusion about love, sex, drugs, and alcohol are all challenges that girls are facing at younger and younger ages. Today's horrific rate of sexual violence against girls, abuse and neglect, eating disorders, and the heartbreaking rate of suicide should be a clear indication of the spiritual attack young women are under. Single moms, it's imperative to know that your children are *thirty-three times* more likely to suffer serious abuse if you have a boyfriend living in the house.[3]

Did You Know?

- Women are routinely degraded in everything from pop culture to casual conversation.
- A girl is bullied every seven minutes in the schoolyard, playground, stairwell, classroom, or bathroom.
- Every fifteen seconds a woman is battered.
- One in three girls who have been in a serious relationship says she has been concerned about being hurt physically by her partner.
- Women are devalued in the workplace, making only seventy-six percent of their male peers' salaries.
- Girls are more likely than boys to be victims of cyberbullying.
- One out of four college-age women have an eating disorder.
- Suicide is the third leading cause of death among adolescents and teenagers. Teen girls are more likely to attempt suicide.
- Women make up nearly fifty-one percent of the population, but hold just sixteen percent of the seats in Congress.
- Three-fourths of girls with low self-esteem engage in negative activities, such as disordered eating, bullying, smoking, or drinking.
- Only two percent of women think they are beautiful.
- One in three girls between the ages of sixteen and eighteen say sex is expected for people their age if they're in a relationship.[4]

Out of the Mire

After that year in Boston, I went back to New York to continue my studies at Pace University. I met a young man and got pregnant not long afterward. I could not believe it; it was our first encounter and the relationship lasted only a short time. I feel so embarrassed that I was literally shocked that I got pregnant so fast. Yes girls, that happens a lot. Make sure you talk to a spiritual adult before participating in any sexual activities, because you really need to count the cost in terms of what it will mean for your body and your soul. To save myself, my future, and my reputation I shamefully chose to have an abortion (the one thing I said I would never do). I was a selfish girl who cared more about what people thought and how things looked than the life growing inside of me.

I was not emotionally or physically prepared for the abortion. Several of my friends had already been through the process and it seemed to be a fairly simple procedure, but for me, it was not.

For me, even just sitting in the waiting room was torture. I could hear the suction machine (the sound was like a very powerful vacuum cleaner) being used on the women before me, and I could hear the cries of the women who were in the recovery room. In my heart, I knew what I was about to do was wrong, but I was such a coward, I chose to go ahead with terminating the pregnancy.

In the procedure room, the provider administered the medication for pain and sedation, and I fell asleep. For some reason I didn't stay asleep. I heard the machine and woke up as they were suctioning the fetus and placenta out. I started crying and screaming because it was at that moment it dawned on me that a precious life was growing inside of me and that it took a surgical instrument with long handles and a long plastic tube connected to a suction device to tear the fetus out of me. I was convinced I was going against God. I was devastated. They gave me more anesthesia and I woke up in the recovery room with a woman (I call her my angel) in the bed next to mine, holding my hand and comforting me. She said that when they brought me in I was crying and repeating, "God will never forgive me for this; I am so sorry." She just held onto my hand and said, "God still loves you, honey, and he will forgive you." She promised she wouldn't leave me until I felt better. I closed my eyes, and when I awoke, I looked around and she was gone. I asked the nurse where the lady in the bed next to mine went, but nobody knew who I was talking about. The nurse said nobody was in the bed next to mine.

I believe God used that situation to wake me up to the depth of my selfishness and that he wanted me to feel the pain of what I had done so I would never forget. At that stage in my life, it had become much too easy to do the things I had said I would never do, and that scared me. I realized that I had hit a new low and that if I did not change, things would get worse. I had become the woman I never wanted to become. I'm sure many of us can relate to this downward spiral.

All I could do was pray, "God, I know you still love me, even though I don't love myself after what I've done." I tried reading the Bible, but because it was the King James Version, I didn't understand it, so I asked, "God, please send people to help me understand the Bible and my purpose here on earth, and this time I will listen. God, you know I love you and only want to follow you to heaven, so please lead me to a great church and, yes, God, please send me some friends I can trust." That really is still my simple prayer today.

DREAM DARE

Dare to forgive and be forgiven.

For Reflection: pray...ponder...promise...practice.

"But when you are praying, first forgive anyone you are holding a grudge against, so that your Father in heaven will forgive your sins, too." (Mark 11:25 NLT)

Chapter Four

He Set My Feet on a Rock

God loves each of us as if there were only one of us. —Augustine

He set my feet on a rock
and gave me a firm place to stand. (Psalm 40:2b)

In May 1985 I was attending Pace University in New York City when, as God would determine it, I was in a class with Kathy Mora, a fellow Aquinite with whom I had served on the Student Council. Kathy reached out to me and invited me to a Bible discussion. This time I went, and at that Bible discussion, I was introduced to Jesus and some men and women who loved him and were striving daily to live like him. It still sends chills up my spine that only two weeks after my prayer asking God to send people to me who could help, I met the girls. Ladies, *know that when you reach out to God, he hears you and comes near to you.* He says to come near to him and he will come near to you (James 4:8).

I am eternally indebted to the mission team sent to New York, led by Steve and Lisa Johnson, and to the lovely ladies who taught me and showed me Jesus. My friends Kathy Mora and Pam Gurentz taught me how to stand on the Rock as they shared the truth from God's word about his love and his desire for me to live according to his word. I shed tears of joy as my heart melted and I found the One I had been searching for all my life. I fell in love with the greatest Love of all. Finally, I would have a firm place to stand, on the Rock!

On May 17, 1985, I went down in the waters of baptism, confessing

Jesus as my Lord and Savior and accepting his gracious gift of salvation. In him I found my true origin, identity, worth, and value. I found the answers and direction I needed to live out God's purpose for my life. All glory to God! I was set free and forgiven of all my past, present, and future sins, and I decided then never to go back to my old life but to trust the plan God had for me as it unfolded.

I can honestly say that as I look back over the last twenty-eight years of my life in Christ, I wouldn't want to imagine it without him. In every stage of life from singlehood to almost empty nester, God has made his paths beyond tracing out (Romans 11:33). Through both the good times and the dreadful, difficult ones, there has been no better place to be than safe in my Father's arms.

Truthfully, my salvation alone is more than I deserved, but God's goodness is boundless. I shared earlier about my parents who were hopeless alcoholics and how the situation seemed impossible. Well, God gets a kick out of working with the impossible. And I think he also takes pleasure in surprises. Just when we think he's forgotten, he's glad to show his glory so no one can boast. Well, God did not forget my family! In June 1999, my dad was diagnosed with stage four stomach cancer. As the cancer spread all over his body, Mike, the kids, and I prayed fervently that Dad would humble himself before the Lord and prepare to meet him. Astonishingly, both Mom and Dad stopped drinking, and in early September of that year, Dad requested that Mike and I visit him in the hospital because he wanted to talk about his relationship with God. After a great talk sharing the Scriptures, God opened Dad's heart to respond to the gospel, embrace God's love, surrender to Jesus, and decide to follow him. He repented and that evening was baptized by Sam Powell and Mike in the only available tub in Beth Israel hospital in Manhattan (at the time all the other tubs where being remodeled). Immediately he was filled with a joy I had never witnessed my dad having before, and like Paul, he immediately started preaching. He began to reach out to the other patients around him, my brother, and the folks who visited him. It took fourteen years of praying for God to soften my dad's heart and for him to humble himself and surrender to Jesus. What a joy it was to spend his last fourteen days with him before God took him home.

Dad was one of Mom's few companions, so his passing left an emptiness in her heart and an openness to build deeper relationships with me and other women like Betty Landergott, Jean Johnson, Camille Khairule, Miriam Quilan, and Mama Marie. Praise God, for twelve years Mama BJ and I had the pleasure of building something I always wanted, a close mother-daughter relationship. Mom sober was always described as kindhearted, thoughtful, and caring, but since she stopped drinking, this personality became ever more apparent and enjoyable. My kids considered her their best friend, and every time she would come to stay with us in Georgia, they slept in her room in her bed or on the floor. Over the years, Mom became more and more open to reading the Bible (not only the Psalms), and through those years my family witnessed her love for God grow and her character reflect his in so many ways. She became the most loving, sacrificial, joyful person I know as she began to meditate and apply the words of Jesus. Mama BJ became probably the most encouraging woman I will ever have the pleasure of knowing and loving. You can read her tribute at the beginning of this book.

In May 2010 Mike and I had the honor of baptizing my seventy-four-year-old mama in the presence of our kids, Alexis and Joe, and many witnesses. In July 2011 God called my precious mom home after she had been diagnosed with pancreatic cancer. I am eternally indebted to my brother who took such good care of my mom, her house, and her every need.

And that's not all; there's more besides. To be sure, every Christian parent's prayer is that their children build their own relationships with Jesus and decide to love him. Mama BJ's conversion had an impact on many people and especially my children, Alexis and Joe. They witnessed Mom truly change, and they watched her courageously suffer through the pain of pancreatic cancer, never complaining, always giving and joyful. Alexis was baptized in August 2011 and Joe in September 2012.

He Put a New Song in My Mouth

> *He put a new song in my mouth,*
> *a hymn of praise to our God.*
> *Many will see and fear the LORD*
> *and put their trust in him.* (Psalm 40:3)

I sing his praises for taking a girl like me from a background like mine and making me into a devoted wife and mother. I praise him for giving me a husband who loves him more than life and unconditionally loves our kids and me. We will celebrate our twenty-third anniversary in September 2013. I praise him for blessing me with two incredible children who love him, Alexis (20) and Joe (18), and for having the pleasure of enjoying Mike's parents and nine siblings.

A Hymn of Praise to Our God

You may recall that I shared earlier about my dream as a child to serve and help people. Well, up to this point in my life I have never gone on a mission to serve the poor in Africa, but I have learned that God had a mission for me right here in my city, in my neighborhood. So often, we miss the mission right before us because we think we have to go to someplace overseas or just different from what we are used to. I believe we are called to make disciples of all nations, so that means some of us will go and some of us will stay, and if we stay, we do what Jesus did. Either way, we are still on a mission.

I praise him for using me over the last twenty-three years to train diverse women of all ages to build intimate relationships with God and embrace his dream for their lives. I praise him for the opportunities to travel throughout the USA and abroad sharing my life and speaking to women who are hungry for him. I praise him for using Mike and me to serve in the full-time ministry as evangelist and women's ministry leader since 1990, first in the New York City Church of Christ in Harlem and the Bronx and currently in the Greater Atlanta Church of Christ. I praise him that he has worked powerfully through us to help countless souls turn to him, remain faithful, rise up to leadership, and spread the gospel around the world. I praise him for building in us a deep conviction and a commitment to passing the torch of leadership to the next generation!

Now I realize that our lives are like a quilt.

Quilt of Life
by Fern Estes

Our life here on earth is much the same
As a beautiful quilt on display.
The pattern is there, we are given the cloth
To form the blocks each day.
As children, we choose the reds and the golds,
The pinks, the blues and the greens.
We have never yet seen the drabness that comes
With the shattering gray of our dreams.
We form the blocks haphazardly
With no thought of hues or design.
It is only when it is half finished
Do we notice the passing of time.

It is then we can see the red and the gold
More beautiful patches of gray.
Just like the darkest nights of our lives
Are made bright by the breaking of day.
As the quilt stretches out in my twilight years
And I add a few stitches each day
I can see the touch of the Master's Hand
As I look at those patches of gray.
Life wasn't meant to be a an array
Of bright colored pinks and blue.
He knew there would be patches of gray
When He gave the pattern to you.[1]

This one thing I know for sure: "In all things God works for the good of those who love him, who have been called according to his purpose" (Romans 8:28).

DREAM DARE

Dare to be grateful for who you are, your family, where God has brought you in life, and what he has in store for your future.

For Reflection: pray…ponder…promise…practice.

King David went in, took his place before God, and prayed: "Who am I, my Master God, and what is my family, that you have brought me to this place in life? But that's nothing compared to what's coming, for you've also spoken of my family far into the future, given me a glimpse into tomorrow, my Master God! What can I possibly say in the face of all this? You know me, Master God, just as I am. You've done all this not because of who I am but because of who you are—out of your very heart!—but you've let me in on it." (2 Samuel 7:18–21 MSG)

Chapter Five

Dare to Be a Wife and Mother of Noble Character

What greater thing is there for two human souls, than to feel that they are joined for life—to strengthen each other in all labor, to rest on each other in all sorrow, to minister to each other in all pain, to be one with each other in silent unspeakable memories at the moment of the last parting? —George Eliot

Making the decision to have a child—it's momentous. It is to decide forever to have your heart go walking around outside your body.
—Elizabeth Stone

Who can find a virtuous and capable wife?
  She is more precious than rubies.
Her husband can trust her,
  and she will greatly enrich his life.
She brings him good, not harm,
  all the days of her life.
She finds wool and flax
  and busily spins it.
She is like a merchant's ship,
  bringing her food from afar.
She gets up before dawn to prepare breakfast for her household
  and plan the day's work for her servant girls.
She goes to inspect a field and buys it;
  with her earnings she plants a vineyard.

She is energetic and strong,
a hard worker.
She makes sure her dealings are profitable;
her lamp burns late into the night.
Her hands are busy spinning thread,
her fingers twisting fiber.
She extends a helping hand to the poor
and opens her arms to the needy.
She has no fear of winter for her household,
for everyone has warm clothes.
She makes her own bedspreads.
She dresses in fine linen and purple gowns.
Her husband is well known at the city gates,
where he sits with the other civic leaders.
She makes belted linen garments
and sashes to sell to the merchants.
She is clothed with strength and dignity,
and she laughs without fear of the future.
When she speaks, her words are wise,
and she gives instructions with kindness.
She carefully watches everything in her household
and suffers nothing from laziness.
Her children stand and bless her.
Her husband praises her:
"There are many virtuous and capable women in the world,
but you surpass them all!"
Charm is deceptive, and beauty does not last;
but a woman who fears the LORD will be greatly praised.
Reward her for all she has done.
Let her deeds publicly declare her praise.

(Proverbs 31:10–31 NLT)

Once upon a time, there lived a wise mother who sat down to share her pearls of wisdom with her young prince who would someday be king. She taught him how to be a godly king and how to find an outstanding wife. Many believe the woman behind this picture of the ideal woman was the mother of King Lemuel. She must have exhibited many of the qualities she described, and she must have known that finding such a woman was rare but not impossible. How else could she teach such priceless pearls of wisdom?[1]

The list of qualities he is to look for in a wife form an alphabetical acrostic poem, with the verses beginning with successive letters of the Hebrew alphabet. Perhaps the author organized the description of an excellent wife this way to help the reader learn this information.[2] It is reassuring that the words of Proverbs 31 were from the lips of a woman about what an excellent woman looks like.

In the past, I was intimidated by her (and I don't think I'm alone) because I was mesmerized by all the things she did well and compared myself to her, only to feel inadequate every time. It finally hit me that I was missing the point. First of all, instead of reading this as "Wow, look at all she accomplished simultaneously," I needed to understand that these were seasons in her life, not necessarily things she did every day. For example, inspecting a field and buying it and planting a vineyard would not be a daily task or even a yearly task—who knows? These are things she did over the course of her lifetime. Also, she had servants and plenty of help. Just goes to show: Don't compare yourself with others; take their examples and apply them in your situation.

That being said, the whole point eluded me. It's not about all the things she did; it's really about who she was. You see, my friends, *"there are many virtuous and capable women in the world."* Women who are honorable, decent, and self-sacrificing abound. There are scores of women who are doing noteworthy things at home and in their careers. There are also women who are making a monumental impact all over this world. Rich and beautiful women are plentiful, but a wife of noble character surpasses them all. The fundamental fact about this ideal woman is that she *"fears the Lord."* Actually, the book of Proverbs begins (1:7) and ends (31:30) with the foundation of life, the fear of the Lord.

God longs for us, as wives and mothers, to first of all revere, honor, stand in awe of, and obey him. This is the woman God praises! When we have hearts like that, we will be enthused and up for the challenge of striving to exemplify the Proverbs 31 woman's attributes in our own lives.

Never underestimate the role of noble wife and mother. If I may be candid, ladies, we are either helping to build up our homes or helping to tear them down, with our own hands.

> *Lady Wisdom builds a lovely home;*
> > *Sir Fool comes along and tears it down brick by brick.* (Proverbs
> 14:1 MSG)

In this chapter we will not have an opportunity to dissect all of this woman's qualities (although I think that would be a great study to do); instead my goal is to touch on a few that may illustrate how God uses us as wives and mothers as a part of his dream for wonderful families. I welcome you to join me as I delve into the treasure of the Proverbs 31 woman and to store a few gems that will assist in building up your home, brick by brick.

The Brick of Virtue

I don't know about you, but when I have run across the word "virtuous," I haven't defined it the way it is used some 200-plus times in the Bible: "to describe an army of men, men of war, and men prepared for war. This Old Testament word refers to a force and is used to mean "able, capable, mighty, strong, valiant, powerful, efficient, worthy, and [having] mental energy."[3] Ruth is described as virtuous. God's woman is astute and a force for good. Do you see the tremendous and dynamic role you have as a wife and mother?

OK, ladies, I'm about to go for it here. Did you notice that the words used to describe this woman's character are "mighty," "strong," and "powerful"? Oftentimes when we attach these words to a woman we think of her being an "independent" woman. I can hear Beyoncé singing her song now:

I depend on me.
All the women who are independent
Throw your hands up at me.[4]

Note to self: the Proverbs 31 sister bestows all her astonishing qualities on others, to build them up and to be the best reflection of God herself. It's not all about her.

The Brick of Value and Self-Worth

A godly wife and mother is like a rare and beautiful treasure. She is worth indefinably more than rubies. No quantity of rare jewels like rubies, corals, and pearls can equal her worth.[5] She must be searched for and sought after. She is the crème de la crème. Dear friend, are you confident of your value and worth? Only when we respect our worth will others respect it.

The Brick of Loving Our Husbands

Let's face it: our families are under attack. Satan's plan is to take parents out so he can devour the children; therefore Mom and Dad must be a strong tower.

It's not a coincidence that the king's mother introduces her description of this noble wife with how she loves her husband. Her respect, encouragement, and steadfast commitment to him and the family enrich his life.

A huge part of loving our husband is being his biggest fan! God expects our husbands to first put their trust in God and then have a safe place of trust within sacred matrimony. A wife of noble character strives to be the most trusted person in her husband's life. She is utterly dependable, loyal, and someone her husband can count on. He can be confident in her integrity and fidelity and in how she handles finances and the family.

I've never been the wife of a husband who does not believe or obey God's word, but I know plenty of them, and I know the following scripture works when wives live it out:

> *In the same way, you wives must accept the authority of your husbands. Then, even if some refuse to obey the Good News, your godly lives will speak to them without any words. They will be won over by observing your pure and reverent lives.* (1 Peter 3:1–2 NLT)

Let's be sure to read through this again. Is God really saying that the non-Christian husband of a Christian wife has authority and the wife is to accept that? YES he is. Remember, he created marriage and knows what works. Here's what I believe: in Ephesians 5:33 God gives us a plan that helps marriages to succeed. He teaches us that the husband must love his wife as he loves himself and that the wife must respect her husband. God knows what women need is LOVE and what men need is LOVE. The way a man feels loved is by being shown respect. Respect is showing adoration, consideration, and esteem. Sometimes wives find it hard to respect their husbands because of all they are not, but every human being deserves respect simply because they were created by God. What works for me is to focus on the positive things I see in my husband and the big and little things he is doing and to praise him for that. Start with #1: He was smart enough to choose you!

I don't know about you, but I like to talk, and I find most women I know like to as well. It's a real challenge when God says your husband won't be won over by your words. Nagging, persuading, yelling, and comparing just won't work. Telling him about what he needs to change and showing him Jesus by your behavior are two very different things. If you are striving to live out the example of Jesus at home, he will be reading the Bible without even picking one up!

A noble wife brings her husband good, not harm *all the days of her life.* This is very convicting to me because it takes a daily focus to bring in the good. There are many opportunities for this, and one way that stands out to me is in our speech. Clearly, this godly woman must have been very encouraging because *"when she speaks, her words are wise, and she gives instructions with kindness."* I don't know about you, but I can tend to be very encouraging with my friends and those outside my home but not always with those inside. Who we are at home is who we really are, so let's daily pray for wisdom and kindness as we daily build up our husbands.

It has been sensational to witness what God has done with one of my best and oldest friends in the world, Amarillis Mercado. I have known her for over eighteen years, and I treasure her as one of my dearest and lifelong friends. She is such a great, stellar example of building up her husband. As she has said, after years of making a lot of excuses, she realized she did not have biblical convictions about her role. She admits to making mistakes, especially during the first three years of marriage, not unlike many of us. She was unaware, reluctant, and unwilling to change, but once she made that simple yet profound decision, "I need to change" and actually put what she learned into practice, God could use her marriage and family to glorify him. It took much prayer, Bible study, studying different resources, and great friends to help her grow, and she is very grateful for all the support through the years.

Who would have imagined that fifteen years later God would use her marriage as an encouragement to so many others? Today her husband, Marcos Mercado, is the Radio One host of *Marriage Beyond the Vows,* a weekly radio show that gives others biblical direction, hope, and inspiration for their relationships. It is broadcast in Philadelphia; South Jersey; Delaware; Charlotte, North Carolina; Detroit, Michigan; and on Black Planet (an online app). Amarillis often joins him on the air and at various events, where they share their lives, their challenges, and what has helped them to overcome. It is evident that they have a great marriage and are devoted to meeting each other's needs and making each other happy.

Our good friends Les and Jean Johnson, who are in their eighties and have been married for sixty years, are known for their simple yet effective marriage counseling. The main thing that they ask is, "Are you making each other happy?" That's it. Simple, right? But think about it: that's not how we usually think. We think, "I married him so he can make me happy." Here's a bombshell: in Gary Thomas's book *Sacred Marriage,* the premise of the book is that the first purpose in marriage, before happiness, sexual expression, the bearing of children, companionship, mutual care and provision, or anything else, is to please God.[6] Marriage is designed to help us get to heaven, so it follows that as you become more holy, you will be happier.

The Brick of Loving Our Children

"I brought you into this world, and I can take you right back out!" "Money does NOT grow on trees!" "If I've told you once, I've told you a thousand times..." "A little birdie told me." "Close the door! You don't live in a barn."

Those are statements that we all may have heard from our moms at one time or another, but on a deeper level, motherhood is about tasting God's capacity to love us. I remember the moments after Alexis was first born and she lay in my arms...I remember absorbing that beautiful and quiet moment, feeling so much love I could hardly imagine being able to love more. As we experience loving our children, even though we love them imperfectly, we come closer to understanding how God loves us with a perfect, unconditional love that always seeks our best interests.

Mothering is such an important role that even Jesus would be born of woman. God knew that Jesus, as a human, had needs as an infant and small child. God gives us mothers to protect, nurture, and mature us. Your mom or some person in that role had the honor of influencing you as you became the person you are. God especially equipped women to meet the need for tenderness, gentleness, and unconditional love, although we all fall short at times and have to learn to give to these needs.

To me, the easy part is having the children; my greatest challenge in life has been teaching them, training them, and loving them so that they flourish, not just grow older. In Proverbs 1, we see that God gives the responsibility to both the father and the mother to instruct and teach the children.

What's profound to me about the Proverbs 31 woman is that she treats all her children in a way that brings forth praise from them. Her love for her family is displayed in the way she carefully watches over everything in her household and is not lazy. Like my mother-in-law, she gets up before dawn to prepare breakfast for her household. That's the truth, friends. When I first married Mike and visited his family in Tallahassee, Florida, one morning I woke up at about 5:00 a.m. to the delicious aroma of food wafting from the kitchen. His mom was preparing breakfast and dinner for that day.

Now when I say the following I want you to hear me out: making the warm clothes and bedspreads for winter was an act of love, not a dreadful duty this woman had to fulfill. Today, I'm afraid too many of us are worried about splitting the household duties fifty-fifty instead of the wife seeing herself as responsible to be the primary caregiver and caretaker of the home. I'm not saying our husbands should not help us at home. Being the primary caretaker does not mean you do everything all by yourself. It means you take responsibility to nurture your family and ensure that the household is taken care of.

Here is a distinguishing characteristic of this woman: although she was a manager of her household, she was not overbearing, lording it over them or being disrespectful. This is of paramount importance because as stated before, a huge way our husbands feel loved is by us respecting them. I believe other people also learn to respect our husbands from the example of respect we give them.

As you can see from the passage, there are many other bricks for building up our homes that we can add here, like the brick of hard work, the brick of industry, the brick of strength and dignity, the brick of fearlessness, the brick of wisdom, and the brick of kindness. The fear of the Lord cements all these bricks together. It has been refreshing for me to finally comprehend that our Proverbs 31 sister is not in the Bible for me to try to reproduce her, but to see her as a call to be the best I can be in my life.

I have many sister friends who live right here in Georgia and all over the country who are commendable wives and mothers. Yolanda Thomas is one of those women who to me truly resemble the heart of the Proverbs 31 woman, and although her life is busy and not always easy, she has prioritized her dreams to have a great marriage, family, and careers.

Shortly after moving to Atlanta, Mike and I were privileged to meet Speech and Yolanda Thomas. Speech is the well-known Grammy Award hip-hop artist who founded the group Arrested Development in the late '80s and made hits like "Tennessee," "People Everyday" (a rewrite of Sly's "Everyday People"), and "Mr. Wendal." Yolanda is his exceptional wife, who deserves a Grammy Award for the way she has managed for fifteen years to prioritize her relationship with God, her husband, and her family while masterfully managing her household, the band, and the side businesses. Her title is CFO, and she refers to herself as the financial diva. She reminds me of what people said about Jesus, that *"he has done everything well."*

Ever since Yolanda Thomas can remember, she always dreamed of being a wife and mother. If you have had the pleasure of meeting her parents, you know why. Willie and Sandra Middleton have been married forty-five years, and Yolanda really enjoyed watching their idyllic relationship grow. She decided she wanted the same for herself. Her mom is a real-life *"wife of noble character,"* and her dad is Sandra's gregarious husband who *"has full confidence in her."* Both have made a lasting impression on Yolanda as well as many of us who know them.

Incredibly, Yolanda's dreams came true when she met Speech in 1991 at a post office in Fayetteville, Georgia. He invited her to be in a music video; she respectfully declined but called him later.

Recalling the nuggets of wisdom her mom had given her growing up, Yolanda could not help but notice how Speech pampered his mom. According to Sandra, that was a reflection of how he would treat Yolanda. Yolanda knew she was in love when she saw how sweet, affectionate, and attentive Speech was with his mom.

Fast forward to seventeen years later, and their journey has been comprised of many ups and some downs, but overall it's been an amazing ride. Yolanda feels very honored that God has allowed her to grow with her wonderful man, to love him, take care of him, and help get him to heaven.

As you can imagine, being married to a star has its benefits and challenges, and I have admired Yolanda's devotion, self-denial, and gigantic and humble heart. I have also learned a lot from her during my kids' teen years, because she has the endearing quality of a quiet and gentle spirit, a quality it is hard to have sometimes during those years.

With her effervescent spirit, she makes her own kids feel undeniably special, and with that same spirit, when the band tours she has opened her arms to the poor of different communities, to orphanages, and to shelters for battered women and children. Likewise, when Speech and Yolanda are not traveling they open their home and consistently share it with children who visit or stay with them temporarily.

Currently, Yolanda has started her own business called Yogi Juice. She has been juicing for the last fifteen years, but when her dad took ill, causing a lack of appetite, Yolanda focused on creating different restorative recipes to help him heal. After juicing for just a few weeks, Yolanda's dad was on the road to recovery. God used that situation to give her a vision for what she could do to help more people. Her passion, Yogi Juice is now a year old, has grown to service loyal, influential clientele all over Georgia, and has been looking to expand. Yolanda is a disciple, wife, mother, and businesswoman who dares to dream!

_____ DREAM DARE _____

Dare to give your heart, mind, energy and resources to build up a household that glorifies God.

For Reflection: pray…ponder…promise…practice.

The wise woman builds her house,
but with her own hands the foolish one tears hers down.

(Proverbs 14:1)

Chapter Six

Dare to Be an Older Woman
Living an Honorable Life

Grow old along with me! The best is yet to be. —Robert Browning

You don't stop laughing because you grow old. You grow old because you stop laughing. —Michael Pritchard

Similarly, teach the older women to live in a way that honors God. They must not slander others or be heavy drinkers. Instead, they should teach others what is good. These older women must train the younger women to love their husbands and their children, to live wisely and be pure, to work in their homes, to do good, and to be submissive to their husbands. Then they will not bring shame on the word of God. (Titus 2:3–5 NLT)

Those of you who know my husband, Mike, know he has a saying, "It takes a decade." He is usually referring to the time it takes to actually get to know and understand your spouse and really connect with them, his point being that there are some things you will only learn through time and experience.

Paul sent the instructions above to Titus so that the older women of the community would understand that they had a grave responsibility. Titus 2 describes the qualities of a godly older woman. Her public and private behavior is respectable and honorable. She is teachable herself, sound in doctrine, and self-controlled, with a purity of heart and a willingness to teach what is good. I can't express how big the need is, especially now, for older women to embrace our role. Younger women need to see the example of our outward behavior reflecting our inward reverence for God. Mature women are to teach and train by our example of conversation, attitude, purity, appearance, submission, and all that is good. We are to train the younger women to love their husbands and children, to be wise, pure, and submissive. Basically, we are to train the young women in LIFE.

Every phase of life is different, brings along its own unique joys and set of challenges, and is a stage in which God can use us abundantly. When I was an unmarried young woman, I was granted divine favor to have the marvelous opportunity to meet the real Jesus and devote all my time and resources to helping others know him. I also struggled a great deal with my insecurity, jealousy, self-control, and purity. As a young married woman I savored sharing my life with my new love and with two of the most beautiful and happy babies ever. My struggles were overcoming selfishness, learning to sacrificially love my husband and children, and learning to trust God and this new husband. A big thing for me was learning to willingly submit to his leadership of me and our household. As a mother of teenagers, God took me to an even deeper level of surrender, trust, unconditional love, faith, and patience (praise God!).

Truthfully, my life would not be what it is today if it weren't for the grace of God and the older women such as my mom, my mother-in-law, Renee Hughes, Cynthia Powell, Lisa Johnson, Amanda Burke, Rhonda Tinnin, and Stacy Fridley who trained and taught me along my journey how to love my husband, children, and people in general. I owe a debt of gratitude to Cynthia Powell for the years of training in marriage, motherhood, and ministry. Her living example, friendship, and words of wisdom imparted to me during our years together changed the trajectory of my life and continue to impact me, my family, and those I influence.

I would also like to acknowledge Lisa Johnson, an inspiring example of a woman who has for many years dared to dream big because her God is a big God. I am so thankful for Lisa's passion, love, faith, and friendship and am especially grateful for her influence in my life. She is one of the main women whose vision for me and so many others inspired us to be the dreamers we are today. Thank you, Lisa!

Many other distinguished women have left an indelible impression on my life. They probably have no idea how much they have influenced the way I think and live: women like Debbie Wright from New York, who displayed genuine love for families and children. Like Anita Banadyga from Portland, who exuded a joyful and encouraging spirit every time I saw her.

She has the gift of making you feel like she's your biggest fan. Like Madie Meeks, who is a woman of noble character and is clothed with strength and dignity. Since I met her, she has continually sought ways to comfort me in my grief, mentor me professionally, and cheer me on in the ministry. Women like Michelle Davis who's life has been faithfully dedicated to loving and nurturing her family through unexplainable chronic illness. She is a loyal loving friend with whom I have shared many tears and roaring laughter and her determination to help people outside of her family inspires me as well. Women like Edie Garmon, who is a woman of faith and prayer and has set an inspiring example of one who has weathered many storms and not given up. Like Beverly Burroughs, Margaret McCants, Jean Johnson, Lupe Mercado, and Betty Landergott, who have that spitfire Caleb spirit. And last but not least, women like Ms. Marie Williams and the Bronx hospital ministry, who comforted my mom during her last months of life.

As I gracefully venture into a new decade, I am actually experiencing more peace, more security, and much more joy than I did in my twenties. I understand better who God made me to be and what I have to give. In this stage in life, I am engaged in the most intimate relationship with God I have ever had. My relationship with my husband is richer and more loving, and I am relishing the loyal friendships that love has sustained through the years as I foster new ones.

There are many great things about growing older in the Lord. When you have persevered and really matured, you have the opportunity to overcome those things that crippled you in your earlier years. Now we may finally know some things because we have been through a few things and hopefully learned plenty. We have not just read or heard about them, but we have lived them, survived, and even thrived.

> *The glory of the young is their strength;*
> *the gray hair of experience is the splendor of the old.*
> (Proverbs 20:29 NLT)

Now is not the time for me to slow down, unplug, and retire. Now is the time for me to give back to the younger women what I have been given. As an older woman, you have a priceless commodity: experience. God sees our role in his church as crucial and commendable—a must. We are needed, maybe now more than ever, to engage and invest in the women in our sphere of influence. That's why he keeps on molding us. He's not finished with us yet.

And he told them this parable: "The ground of a certain rich man yielded an abundant harvest. He thought to himself, 'What shall I do? I have no place to store my crops.'

"Then he said, 'This is what I'll do. I will tear down my barns and build bigger ones, and there I will store my surplus grain. And I'll say to myself, "You have plenty of grain laid up for many years. Take life easy; eat, drink and be merry."'

"But God said to him, 'You fool! This very night your life will be demanded from you. Then who will get what you have prepared for yourself?'" (Luke 12:19–20)

None of us wants to imitate the heart of this man. Instead of being generous with his resources and a blessing to others, he grew more insatiable for resources and complacent with life. Sadly, he lost everything, when he could have given to others and still enjoyed his life as well.

It is important for us to face the fact that just because we passionately lived out our purpose for God at one time in our lives *does not mean that we still do.* As I have gotten older, I have experienced that it is fairly easy to become consumed with the daily responsibilities of life and all the new challenges that come as we age, and as a result experience a lack of passion of our own. If you have lost your passion, don't try to hide behind anything or anyone or make an excuse for it. Face it and be willing to go back to your first love (Revelation 2:4).

These days, I find it even more necessary to be deliberate about this and not merely to talk about and settle for what God has already done, but to continue to believe, put forth action, and wait in expectation of what God will do. Respect the past; expect the future! I feel urgent about shaking off any temptation to tolerate my faith becoming stale, making me reserved and fearful of daring to dream. I refuse to believe that radical, risk-taking faith is only for the young! No matter what age or stage, God never stops dreaming for you.

We need that good ole Caleb spirit:

"So here I am today, eighty-five years old! I am still as strong today as the day Moses sent me out; I'm just as vigorous to go out to battle now as I was then. Now give me this hill country that the LORD promised me that day. You yourself heard then that the Anakites were there and their cities were large and fortified, but, the LORD helping me, I will drive them out just as he said." (Joshua 14:10b–12a)

Are you as vigorous now as you were then, or are your best days in the past?

Perhaps the seven-year stint my husband and I did learning to lead the Bronx teen ministry instilled in us a passion for raising up the next generation. If there's one thing young people hunger for, it's a purpose for living.

Suicide is a serious public health problem that affects even young people. For youths between the ages of ten and twenty-four, suicide is the third leading cause of death. It results in approximately 4,600 lives lost each year. Deaths from youth suicide are only part of the problem. More young people survive suicide attempts than actually die. Each year, approximately 157,000 youth between the ages of ten and twenty-four receive medical care for self-inflicted injuries at emergency departments across the USA.[1] Even as I was proofing this chapter I received news of another young person in his early twenties who committed suicide. This battle is real, ladies!

Reaching out to the children and young adults, not only in our homes but also in and outside of our communities, is a matter of life or death for some of them. My passion is raising up the next generation of women willing to be used by God in whatever capacity he chooses. I am so grateful that Mike has vision for me and the women in our ministry; he sees that women have distinct needs and that there are women who are equipped to meet them. I'm glad that he believes in me and my God-given ability to train women to train other women. Over the years, it has been my pleasure for God to use me to train younger women to love their families and impact others. I've also had the privilege to train several women who have gone into the full-time ministry, like Christina Maldonado, and others who have full-time jobs but full-time-ministry hearts, like Ann Coleman, soon to be PhD and currently changing many lives in our singles ministry. And it has been miraculous to witness countless women who are influencing other single women for Christ on the job or at school.

Leave Your Legacy

My hero Betty Landergott is another one of the reasons I wrote this book. She is absolutely a quintessential woman of God and an esteemed matriarch in our church family. Mike and I had the pleasure of meeting her when she came to the GACC in 2007 with Les and Jean Johnson. Our church was in the beginning stages with about forty members. Betty was in her late sixties and lived in Kennesaw, Georgia, and we were meeting in Buckhead. If she joined us she would travel many miles to and fro, have to build all new relationships, and be in a group with mostly young people and people young in the faith who were predominantly a different race. Who does that these days? Who does what's not comfortable for them because they believe they still have a dream? Who moves into a ministry because there is a need, versus moving into a ministry to get their needs met? Who looks for a church to help build up in whichever area, be it the singles ministry, worship team, or the children's ministry, versus finding a church where everything is set and all they have to do is come?

With deep-rooted convictions about the Bible being the standard and an abounding love for God, his people, and the lost, Betty joined our singles ministry. Over the last eight years, she has given her money to fund interns, served on the church board, and helped numbers of people become Christians. She now serves as part of a shepherding group. Although she is one of our most mature members and has been in the Lord's church longer than any of us, she is also the most humble and respectful. Our two evangelists, Mike and Angel, have often commented about how encouraging, positive, supportive, and respectful Betty has been for as long as they have known her. She has never made a negative remark to them, never had a disrespectful tone or look, and instead of trying to always control things in the ministry, Betty chooses to pray, pray, pray. This is very convicting to those of us women who tend to think we always know what's best. Yikes!

Betty attends church every time the church meets, teaches classes, and is never lacking in zeal. Currently she is a retired teacher in her seventies, still passionately in love with God and on the front line of the battle to seek and save the lost and to help train young Christians in our church. She lays down her life to serve people in her home, and she willingly drives wherever to spend time with the body. After many years, when others have given up, she is still living by faith. Betty is deeply loved by all of us and I guess the highest compliment I can give her is that we all want to be like her.

Betty's Story

I was married at twenty years old and by twenty-six, I wound up divorced and the mother of two small children. Growing up, I was verbally abused, sexually abused by my brother, and neglected. In my marriage, I suffered from physical and emotional abuse. As I got older, I was looking for love in all the wrong places and my search led me to an affair. I found myself pregnant by the affair, in shame and in pain, standing before a judge at midnight holding my son in my arms and being deemed an unfit mother. That night I watched a strange woman take him from my arms. I was never able to regain custody.

But at twenty-six years old I found God. I found the God of the impossible, the God who moves mountains, stills every storm, heals the brokenhearted, and deeply loves sinful women like me.

When I found God, I had a dream that everyone would fall in love with the GOD OF THE IMPOSSIBLE. I wanted to move and take that message to South Korea, then to London, then Singapore, then Bangkok. Every time, God said "No." I learned to trust God's "No." I learned to trust his timing. The son who at four was taken from my arms was baptized at twenty-five and is now in the arms of God. The daughter born of the affair was baptized at twelve. And finally, when the GACC announced taking a team to Bermuda to support our brother Alex who had to move back to his home, at seventy-one I said, *"Here am I. Send me."*

I learned to trust God's dream for me instead of my dream for me; I learned to believe he had a much greater dream for me than I had! No matter where life's journey takes me, I will keep living God's dream for me. I am living God's dream for me right now, right here in Atlanta, Georgia, with the young singles ministry, searching out and helping anyone and everyone who wants the God of the impossible.

I am Betty Landergott and I dare to dream!

Although Betty has her own adult children, she mothers many in our ministry. Anne Coleman is one of her very special "daughters." This is her story:

God Sets the Lonely in Families

Anne's Story

One of the consistent statements I heard growing up was, "Don't trust anybody with your life." As I moved into my adult years, that statement became my motto. I'd perfected the art of being a social butterfly but not having any close friends. From the outside looking in, I was always talking and serving people, but in reality, I never trusted anyone enough to share my life with them. My nuclear family (my parents and my brother) were the only people I trusted. In my heart, there was a tug-of-war as I dreamed of having deep friendships but also took pride in how not having them protected me from drama and heartbreak. I decided to believe what I grew up hearing, and that resulted in a lonely life. Playing it safe was pulling me away from all the amazing things God had in store for me.

In 2001, I started attending the University of Florida. At the time, I was excited about being a Gator and experiencing the college life. In my freshman year, I started to study the Bible, and so many scriptures challenged me to make life changes. I fell in love with God, and for the first time I started learning how to trust. I learned that trusting people has to start with trusting God. At that time of my life, it was easy to dream. My dreams were of going into a PhD program, getting married, and helping people fall in love with God.

Little did I know that the time would soon come when I would face the most difficult challenge of my life. In 2004 my mother, who battled with diabetes and pulmonary hypertension, passed away. My world was shattered and my heart was broken. Before she passed, she and I had become best friends. We would talk on the phone for hours. She knew just by me saying, "Hello" whether I was having a good or bad day. I trusted her with everything in me; I loved her more than I can ever describe in words. When she passed, the trust I had built for God started to fade away. After a while, my heart was so broken that I started to build bitter and angry feelings toward God. For months, I wrestled with thoughts and feelings of anxiety, depression, loneliness, and discouragement. On top of all these feelings, because I did not allow myself to receive God's comfort through other women around me, I isolated myself, putting me in a situation where Satan would ultimately try to destroy me spiritually.

Six months after I graduated, I decided to move to Atlanta, Georgia. I was excited about the new chapter in my life. My drive to Atlanta was very emotional; my little Mazda Protégé was packed with my belongings as I got on I-75 to embrace a new stage in life. On the road, I grabbed one of my Bible Experience CDs (audio readings of the Bible). It started in Judges and went into the book of Ruth. I grew up hearing the story of Ruth, but this time was different. While driving and listening, I heard: *"But Ruth replied, 'Don't urge me to leave you or to turn back from you. Where you go I will go, and where you stay I will stay. Your people will be my people and your God my God'"* (Ruth 1:16). My heart dropped, and I started crying tears of joy. At that time, I could not put it into words, but now I can say Ruth having a Naomi in her life was something I desired. I cried because I felt like I had that in my mom and I was still mourning that loss. After listening to the passage, I started to dream about God giving me a Naomi, a spiritual woman in my life who would love and help me in all aspects of my life.

A year after I moved to Atlanta, a few of the single women and I got together to plan a brothers' appreciation dinner. We wanted to keep the dinner very simple; most of us were just learning how to cook. Out of nowhere, I got a note from Betty saying she wanted to help with the dinner. She cooked an amazing dinner, and the brothers loved it. The sisters loved it even more (it was better than what any of us could have come up with). After the dinner, Betty and I talked over lunch, laughing about the fun times at the dinner. Before I knew it, our lunch times were consistent. I loved and still cherish my times with Betty. I could tell her anything. I started to trust her and loved getting her input. After some months, Betty told me, "You are like a daughter to me." I just looked at her and smiled. She had no idea what those words meant, but I knew it. That was God helping me to see that he made my dreams come true. In my relationship with Betty, God had provided a Naomi for me. A few years later, Betty walked down the aisle as my mom at my wedding. What I love most about my relationship with Betty is that she loves me so unconditionally and allows me to not only sit and learn, but also to serve when the opportunity arrives.

I not only learned to open my heart to Betty, but to so many other women. My friend Dr. Robin Nelson has encouraged me in my academics. I thank her and countless others who have helped me during this PhD program despite my learning disability. The awesome thing is that I had the opportunity to help Dr. Nelson become a Christian, as she has helped me in my academic journey.

I am grateful to God for placing dreams on my heart for my family. My brother, Samuel Magloire, is one of the lives my husband and I dreamed would one day follow Jesus, and we were able to help him become a Christian a little over a year ago.

I've learned to simply trust in God and patiently wait. In that, I have witnessed not just my personal dreams come true but also have been a part of helping other people's dreams come true as well.

I'm so grateful for the Pattersons, who had the vision that one day we would have a vibrant singles ministry at the Greater Atlanta Church of Christ. In just a few years' time, the ministry grew from sixteen people to over 100 disciples. Out of the singles ministry we have eight newlywed couples and several on the horizon. I am convinced that this would not have been possible without men and women who dream for it, pray for it, and work toward it, and I am thankful to God for putting me around other dreamers who call each other higher.

_____ **DREAM DARE** _____

Dare to keep your spiritual fervor, serving the Lord even when you are old and gray.

For Reflection: pray...ponder...promise...practice.

Even when I am old and gray,
do not forsake me, my God,
till I declare your power to the next generation,
your mighty acts to all who are to come. (Psalm 71:18)

Chapter Seven

Dare to Dream When Your Heart Is Broken

God never wastes a hurt! In fact, your greatest ministry will most likely come out of your greatest hurt. —Rick Warren, The Purpose-Driven Life

Although the world is full of suffering it is full also of the overcoming of it. —Helen Keller

Now a man named Lazarus was sick. He was from Bethany, the village of Mary and her sister Martha. (This Mary, whose brother Lazarus now lay sick, was the same one who poured perfume on the Lord and wiped his feet with her hair.) So the sisters sent word to Jesus, "Lord, the one you love is sick."

When he heard this, Jesus said, "This sickness will not end in death. No, it is for God's glory so that God's Son may be glorified through it." Now Jesus loved Martha and her sister and Lazarus. So when he heard that Lazarus was sick, he stayed where he was two more days, and then he said to his disciples, "Let us go back to Judea."

On his arrival, Jesus found that Lazarus had already been in the tomb for four days. Now Bethany was less than two miles from Jerusalem, and many Jews had come to Martha and Mary to comfort them in the loss of their brother. When Martha heard that Jesus was coming, she went out to meet him, but Mary stayed at home.

"Lord," Martha said to Jesus, "if you had been here, my brother

would not have died. But I know that even now God will give you whatever you ask."

Jesus said to her, "Your brother will rise again."

Martha answered, "I know he will rise again in the resurrection at the last day."

Jesus said to her, "I am the resurrection and the life. The one who believes in me will live, even though they die; and whoever lives by believing in me will never die. Do you believe this?"

"Yes, Lord," she replied, "I believe that you are the Messiah, the Son of God, who is to come into the world."

After she had said this, she went back and called her sister Mary aside. "The Teacher is here," she said, "and is asking for you." When Mary heard this, she got up quickly and went to him. Now Jesus had not yet entered the village, but was still at the place where Martha had met him. When the Jews who had been with Mary in the house, comforting her, noticed how quickly she got up and went out, they followed her, supposing she was going to the tomb to mourn there.

When Mary reached the place where Jesus was and saw him, she fell at his feet and said, "Lord, if you had been here, my brother would not have died."

When Jesus saw her weeping, and the Jews who had come along with her also weeping, he was deeply moved in spirit and troubled. "Where have you laid him?" he asked.

"Come and see, Lord," they replied.

Jesus wept.

Then the Jews said, "See how he loved him!"

(John 11:1–7, 17–36)

The Hebrew word *shabar* means "brokenhearted" and is also translated as to burst, broken into pieces, crushing grief, to rend violently, to wreck, and to shatter.[1]

Today we usually use the term "brokenhearted" to describe someone who has suffered the death of a loved one or even a divorce, breakup, physical separation, betrayal, or romantic rejection. Whatever the cause, the pain of a broken heart is crushing and it is real. In 1997 my dad passed of stomach cancer. As a responsible daughter usually does, I went into a "get-things-done mode," and a few days after the funeral I ended up in my physician's office because I had such bad chest pains I thought I was having a heart attack. The doctor gave me the appropriate tests, and seeing the results, she explained that what I was experiencing was "broken heart syndrome." Yes, ladies, a broken heart is both physically and emotionally real.

> Broken heart syndrome is a temporary heart condition brought on by stressful situations, such as the death of a loved one. People with broken heart syndrome may have sudden chest pain or think they're having a heart attack. These broken heart syndrome symptoms may be brought on by the heart's reaction to a surge of stress hormones. In broken heart syndrome, a part of your heart temporarily enlarges and doesn't pump well, while the remainder of the heart functions normally or with even more forceful contractions.[2]

It was not my first time experiencing my heart being in physical pain and it would not be the last. Over the last few years I have witnessed many of my close friends suffer through gut-wrenching sorrow and agony.

Sadly, as a country, we have undergone monumental grief for the victims of 9/11, the devastation from some of the deadliest hurricanes ever to hit the USA, and the senseless slaughter of college students and innocent children while sitting in their classrooms.

There are many things that perplex us in life and leave us asking the question, "Why?" As human beings, it's only normal to ask why. We have been asking why since we could talk. God made us with brains to think and with a curiosity. But just as we have seen with Eve, our curiosity can get us into a lot of trouble. We have to check ourselves when our "whys" go beyond seeking to understand to demanding to control God or know what he knows. It is inevitable that on this side of heaven we will never fully grasp everything that occurs and most likely we will not have all the answers.

John 11 is chock full of the edifying truth about life: the reality that as long as we are in the flesh, no matter how far from or close to Jesus we are, we will experience pain, suffering, and grief. Mary and Martha are prime examples. Although Mary was the same one who poured perfume on the Lord and wiped his feet with her hair and Martha was the same Martha who busily prepared for his visit and served him, they would still have to face a time of suffering. They were brokenhearted over the sickness and impending death of their dear brother. Of course, they had not a clue about what the Lord had in store for the whole situation. I love the fact that we get to see two women who loved and followed Jesus, grieve; the reason being that there is a misconception that if you are faithful you are not to grieve, but the rest of that scripture says, *"like the rest of mankind, who have no hope"* (1 Thessalonians

4:13). Grief is a natural part of the human experience. We all face grief in a multitude of ways.

These two women are biblical heroes in the faith to me because they were able to face grief while clinging to the knowledge that God still cared about them even as they went through trials and troubles. They have taught me some fundamentals that I strive to cling to when troubles come my way personally and as I comfort others.

Call on Jesus

Obviously, Lazarus was very dear to Mary and Martha. Perhaps he was the sole means of support for them, since the Bible does not say anything about husbands or children. In any case, as their dear brother grew very sick, Mary and Martha called for Jesus and asked for his help. If they needed anybody at that moment, it was Jesus. The Bible describes him as a man of sorrows, and acquainted with grief (Isaiah 53:3 ESV). He was not only able to relate, but also to help. God is our refuge and strength, an ever-present help in trouble (Psalm 46:1). In times of trouble, there may be diverse resources available or suggested to us including psychoanalysis, medication, and time. Those things may very well be needed to address emotions and resolve feelings, but remember: God heals the heart. When we pray, Christians can tap into the power of the Holy Spirit of God who alone *"heals the brokenhearted and binds up their wounds"* (Psalm 147:3). And after all, he is the source of all resources.

Keep It Real

Mary and Martha were grieving and in shock. It all seems to have happened rapidly, and understandably the sisters grappled with grasping it all and why Jesus had not been there sooner. I admire Martha's candor and how she asserts faith in Jesus as the Healer and Savior: *"If you had been here, my brother would not have died."* I can also hear her saying, "Where were you, Jesus? What happened?" I don't know about you, but I have felt that at times: "Where is God?" "Does he see what's going on?" "Doesn't God care?" Yes, he does! God has promised to go through our trials with us.

> *When you pass through the waters, I will be with you;*
> *and through the rivers, they shall not overwhelm you;*
> *when you walk through fire you shall not be burned,*
> *and the flame shall not consume you.* (Isaiah 43:2 ESV)

It's good to be real about what you feel and to remember the undeniable facts that God always has a plan and is always on time and that ultimately his glory is the goal.

Cling to Convictions

Dear friends, it's a good time to examine ourselves and ask how deep our convictions about Jesus are. Do we wholeheartedly believe that Jesus is God in the flesh and is the resurrection and the life? Mary and Martha knew Jesus well because they had a personal relationship with him. If we are going to build deep convictions about Jesus, we have to make time to nurture our personal relationship with our Lord and Savior. Do we recognize his power and believe he is faithful, good and right in all things? All of us will have our conviction tested by the fiery trials in life, even the most faithful of us. Inconceivably, in just one day Job lost his children, nearly all his worldly possessions, his health, and his source of livelihood. Both the magnitude of this calamity and his response to it are flabbergasting to me. *"Then Job arose and tore his robe and shaved his head and fell on the ground and worshiped. And he said, 'Naked I came from my mother's womb, and naked shall I return. The Lord gave, and the Lord has taken away; blessed be the name of the Lord'"* (Job 1:20–21 ESV). Job grieved, tenaciously worshipped God, and endured faithfully. He clung to his convictions. He was human, so at times he doubted God's goodness in these tragic events, but because he persevered through the trials he grew closer to God through God's revelation of himself (Job 42:1–5). Job learned through heartbreak that God is good and always faithful.

Be Comforted by God and Others

First, it's consoling to know that God is always near to comfort his people: *"He is near to the brokenhearted and saves the crushed in spirit"* (Psalm 34:18 ESV); *"Blessed be the God and Father of our Lord Jesus Christ, the Father of mercies and God of all comfort"* (2 Corinthians 1:3 ESV).

Second, it's reassuring to know that God's grace enables us to bear all trouble.

> *But He said to me, My grace (My favor and loving-kindness and mercy) is enough for you [sufficient against any danger and enables you to bear the trouble manfully]; for My strength and power are made perfect (fulfilled and completed) and show themselves most effective in [your] weakness. Therefore, I will all the more gladly glory in my weaknesses and infirmities, that the strength and power of Christ (the Messiah) may rest (yes,*

may pitch a tent over and dwell) upon me! (2 Corinthians 12:9 AMP)

Third, it's heartening to know that we are not alone. Those who came to comfort Mary were weeping along with her. That kind of compassion moved Jesus deeply, and he wept too. Jesus wept? Yes, when grief came, Jesus was vulnerable and not afraid or too proud to express the feeling inside. Real men do cry! God gave us tear glands to use when we need them. During my mom's illness, it seemed as though I cried many buckets full of tears. It was devastating to watch her in excruciating pain as the cancer ravaged her body and tumors protruded from her spine. It got to the point that I would try to hold back the tears because of the headaches I would suffer from afterward, but almost always I would feel better after a good cry. Not suppressing emotions can be healthy, and weeping together can bring comfort to the hurting soul. As the saying goes, it takes both rain and sunshine to make a rainbow.

In 1990 God sent Mike and me to serve the Harlem ministry. Our years in Harlem will forever be etched on our hearts because of the faith, hope and love we experienced from the people and the miraculous things God did with us as a church family. Harlem is where I learned that love never fails, God's grace is sufficient for me, and his power is made perfect in my weakness. I also learned servant leadership. I remember that time as one of the best times in my life. I remember those people as some of the greatest disciples I have ever known.

One of those mighty warriors has been a loyal friend to me and my family ever since. The American artist Barbara Bloom once noted, "When the Japanese mend broken objects, they aggrandize the damage by filling the cracks with gold. They believe that when something's suffered damage and has a history it becomes more beautiful." That's how I see Irene. By persevering through many trials, Irene Rivera exemplifies the Father of compassion and the God of all comfort. She is so beautiful.

Irene's Story

When I found that my teenage son had died in his sleep, I thought my heart was going to stop. The sorrow was so overwhelming I had to remember to breathe. I was living a mother's worst nightmare—my son, my baby boy, my only child was suddenly gone. My heart was crushed and I thought I was going to die.

On that day, August 1, 2003, I became a woman of heart-wrenching sorrow. As the EMTs and police officers asked me questions, I kept hoping it was all a bad dream. It had to be a nightmare. I would wake up often, hearing Manuel's voice telling me he was ready to go buy his custom-designed skateboard. But it was not a dream.

My relationship with my son was unique—we were a team. He knew that I loved him deeply and that I would crawl through broken glass to protect him and to keep him safe.

After Manuel's death, the days blended together. Many tears were shed as family and friends came by to pay their respects, yet I remained in utter shock. I remember asking God "What did I do so wrong that you would take my only child?" I kept replaying that fateful morning over and over in my mind as if somehow I could figure out a way to have things end differently. The sorrow was consuming and the grief unbearable. I was not able to eat or sleep, and I was inconsolable.

Deep in my heart, I knew I wasn't the only one mourning, but that was little comfort when I entered his room and realized I would never again hear his voice. Never again would I be able to help him with his hair or iron his T-shirts, or cook him his favorite meal of beef stew. A mother should never have to pick out the last outfit her son will wear and take it to the funeral parlor. During those first few months, dark thoughts constantly filled my heart and mind.

One of my best friends who flew in from Texas shared Isaiah 42:16 with me before the wake, and it snapped me out of the automatic-pilot mode that I had been in: *"I will lead the blind by ways they have not known, along unfamiliar paths I will guide them; I will turn the darkness into light before them and make the rough places smooth."* God knew that I would only have Manuel for seventeen years on earth. He put this scripture in the Bible to comfort me and help me through the pain and sorrow. God completely understood my feelings of loss and despair. Even when I did not know how I felt, God understood and his word brought me comfort.

As expected, the first year after Manuel's death was full of "rough places." I would not only deeply miss his presence; I would miss everything about him. I would hear his voice calling me "Mami." Even receiving college applications addressed to him made me cry a lot. God himself, through his word, helped me to remain faithful that year. At that time I had to constantly pray, "God, I don't understand why Manuel had to die, but I trust that you love me and that your way is perfect...help me, because I feel blind, I feel lost; please make these rough places smooth." To this day, I still pray those prayers when I need to embrace my fear of loss and suffering.

Through God's mercy and grace, I chose to believe that God is faithful to all his promises. He had faith in me and I choose every day to be faithful to him. For me, the loss took my faith and trust to a deeper place in my relationship with him.

God promised that he would be with me, heal me, and restore to me the joy of salvation (Psalm 51:12). He promised that he would comfort me, and most of all, he promised I would see Manuel again. I made a conscious decision to cling to God. It was not easy; I wrestled often with dark thoughts of doubt and anger toward God during my mourning. In order to fight off those evil accusations, I had to remind myself of the truth found in God's word.

During my time of grief, I had no idea that God would have a purpose for my pain. My faithfulness through Manuel's death has given me countless opportunities to reach out to others in pain and share their burdens. The jewels of wisdom, the scars of suffering, and the tears of sorrow were not meant to be wasted. God's dream for me was to use them as a banner and shield to help others overcome their despair. Twenty-four years ago when I first made Jesus Lord, I would never have said, "My kingdom dream is to suffer so that I can comfort those who suffer."

I would have never chosen this, but God has worked through my sorrow for my good, and that has been more fulfilling than what I could have ever expected. My sorrow became balm for the souls of others. As God held me together during this painful ordeal, I became the example of faith for others. Over time I became the "death expert," the "go-to person" if there was a death or chronic illness. The comfort I received from God and others began to flow through me to those in pain or suffering. This not only gave me new purpose, but it also encouraged my spirit to grow in faith and wisdom while surrendering to God's plan and his dream for my life.

As I learned day by day to trust God with my "whys" and my emotional pain, I still prayed. Prayer is a reminder that I need God through all the questions that can still torture me. My grief will be ever present; I will never see my son graduate or get married. I will never hold a grandchild in my arms. My loss is ever before me, but so is my almighty God.

Fourteen months after Manuel's death, my mother, Anna, passed away. I remember the conversation with my youngest brother when I called him to tell him she had passed. He asked me if I wanted him to take charge of the arrangements. I told him no, that I had learned so much with

Manuel's funeral that I didn't mind—he could take care of the next one. And so it was—another death to mourn, more people to comfort, more lives that could be changed.

The year after my mother passed, I buried one of my best friends who died of colon cancer. Since that time, I have had the opportunity to comfort numerous friends diagnosed with breast cancer and other grave or terminal illnesses. I have visited more hospitals than I can count and helped plan many more funerals than I ever expected. All the while, God knew that this was the road I would travel for him. I have been blessed through this situation with amazing relationships and spiritual fruit, for out of tragic events God can and will be glorified.

_____ DREAM DARE _____

Dare to let God impart to you life after loss.

For Reflection: pray...ponder...promise...practice.

"You're blessed when you feel you've lost what is most dear to you. Only then can you be embraced by the One most dear to you." (Matthew 5:4 MSG)

Chapter Eight

Dare to Use Your Talents Wisely

Every person must have a concern for self, and feel a responsibility to discover one's mission in life. God has given each normal person a capacity to achieve some end. True, some are endowed with more talent than others, but God has left none of us without talent. Potential powers of creativity are within us, and we have a duty to work assiduously to discover these powers.

—Dr. Martin Luther King Jr.

Our talents are the gift that God gives to us; what we make of our talents is our gift back to God — Leo Buscaglia

Everyone Has a Talent

Every human being, regardless of their belief in God or in Christ, is given at least one natural talent with different variations and degrees as a result of a combination of factors. Talents are features that give every human being a unique personality. Natural talents come from God. He is the giver of *"every good and perfect gift,…coming down from the Father of the heavenly lights, who does not change like shifting shadows"* (James 1:17).

One of my favorite reality series is *America's Got Talent*. Performers of all ages come from across the USA ready to showcase their talent. They sing, dance, juggle, do magic, and a variety of other things, all vying for their chance to strut their stuff and perform on stage. The big hope is to win the country's hearts and the one-million-dollar prize.

It's obvious that some people are multitalented and others maybe not, but be encouraged, my friends: we all have talent and possibly talent waiting to be discovered. God gives us what we can handle. For instance, I know I could not handle Mariah Carey's talent. My head would be so swollen with pride I wouldn't be able to lift it off the bed. In my opinion, Mariah Carey is one of the best female singers of all time. Her five-octave voice serenades us. Her talent is undeniable; it is uniquely displayed in her range, her pitch, and her power when hitting those high notes and how she makes it all look so easy. We'd be hard pressed to find a soul who would not agree that Michael Jackson was the greatest entertainer of all time. The amount of talent he embodied just seemed boundless. No matter how many can imitate his moves, there was only one MJ.

That's exactly how God feels about *you!* No matter how many talents you have and what they are, there is only one you; therefore, what you have to bring to the table will be uniquely special and needed. As we know, you don't have to be a superstar to be supertalented. Our dear brother, Jodi Lewis, was a member of the GACC since its inception. His title could have been music minister, but he didn't have a title; he was just Jodi. He led our singing with more passion and conviction than anyone else I know did. God ministered to our hearts through him as he poured his heart out in song, inspiring us to do so also. He has gone on to Paradise now, is deeply loved and missed, and will forever be treasured in our hearts. Thanks, Jodi, for leaving the words to one of your favorite songs on our hearts: "There's no other name that's higher than yours, Lord."

My own mom had amazing natural talents and abilities. I mentioned earlier that she was legally blind, completely deaf in one ear, and losing her hearing in the other. In spite of all her challenges, she not only could play the piano and sing, but she also had perfect pitch. As her sight grew worse, she learned to play by ear with the little hearing she had left. I remember playing "Sukiyaki" by Rokusuke Ei (A Taste of Honey made it to number 3 in the USA with their English lyric version in 1981) on the record player (I'm dating myself), and the next thing I knew, Mom was playing it on the piano, singing, "It's all because of you I'm feeling sad and blue." Mom had a tremendous amount of natural talent and ability.

Less celebrated at times are talents like being a great homemaker (Ruth), a maker of clothes (Dorcas), a tentmaker (Priscilla), intelligent (Abigail), a bargain shopper, an engineer, a teacher, or a great listener able to connect. The list of talents is endless.

Are You a 'Natural'?

If you are a good athlete, for example a great basketball player, consider where all your talent came from. Maybe you think, "I'm just a 'natural.' God didn't need to give me anything; I already had the ability. I did it all myself." If that is what you think, your ignorance is matched only by your arrogance. Where do you think your ability ultimately came from? Are you the one who determined your genetic make-up? Did you make the arrangements for your upbringing? Were you the one who worked it out to be born in a nation where you would have plenty of opportunities to train, instead of having to work fifteen hours a day from an early age? Did you provide the food to strengthen you in childhood and the nutrients and immunizations to fend off the disease which could have crippled you?

How many of these advantages are you taking credit for? Are you so sure you want to eliminate the Lord from your analysis? Even a "natural" has been well endowed and endued by God. Of course, no one says, "Michael Jordan [even though he is a 'superhero'] plays supernaturally. He shouldn't be allowed to compete—he has God helping him." But there is some truth in that last statement: Every good thing "M.J." has, God has given him—directly or indirectly. And the same applies to you and me! There's no such thing as a "self-made man." As Paul said, *"For who makes you different from anyone else? What do you have that you did not receive? And if you did receive it, why do you boast as though you did not?"* (1 Corinthians 4:7).[1]

You are the director of the talents God has given to you. No matter how you see your talents, God requires *"that those who have been given a trust must prove faithful"* (1 Corinthians 4:2). Your talents are not given to you to be used selfishly just to make money, to make you more comfortable, and to retire; they are to benefit others. If you miss that point, you miss the point of why you are on this earth. *"Each one should use whatever gift he has received to serve others, faithfully administering God's grace in its various forms"* (1 Peter 4:10 NIV 1984).

Just know that if you faithfully use your talents for God, there's no telling how much more he will do in you, as Jesus taught in his parable: *"Well done, good and faithful servant! You have been faithful with a few things; I will put you in charge of many things. Come and share your master's happiness"* (Matthew 25:21).

If you hone your craft, there's no telling what doors God will open and before which "kings" you will serve: *"Do you see someone skilled in their work? They will serve before kings; they will not serve before officials of low rank"* (Proverbs 22:29).

In today's "serve-me" society, we as true Christians need to be very careful that this serve-me attitude does not characterize us. My Bible says in Matthew 20:28 that *"the Son of Man did not come to be served, but to serve, and to give his life as a ransom for many."* Let's reflect on that a moment: the Son of Man's whole purpose was to serve and to give his life.

What would the church be like if more Christians really had this mind-set? I mean really. What if when we looked at other people and loved them, we thought of what we could give to them instead of what we could get out of them? What if every Christian really decided to use his or her gifts to build up the body instead of just enjoying the benefits of having others use their gifts? How about if in relationships, instead of looking for who we think could really meet our needs we looked for whom we could give to as well, for mutual encouragement? In marriages, how about we compete to out-serve each other? What a blast that is! What if whatever door we walked through (church, home, school, work) our first thought was "How can I serve?" We all want to be a "great" but are we all willing to be a great servant? Jesus said, *"Whoever wants to become great among you must be your servant, and whoever wants to be first must be your slave"* (Matthew 20:26–27).

Since the church is full of talented people, it would make sense that it would be a place where Christians could use their talents and that the talents in the church would benefit the church as well as the world. It's disheartening when I see Christians use all their talent in the world but refuse to use it to serve the church. I understand some of us may have what we think are legitimate reasons for not doing so, but I'm just asking, if Jesus gave his life for the church, what's a good excuse to not give her our talent?

In 2009 our church hosted our first Arts and Entertainment conference here in Atlanta, Georgia. The A&E conference brings international artists and entertainers from the following industries together: radio, broadcasting, film and TV acting, modeling, Internet media, writing, public speaking, sports, entertainment law, gaming, graphic design, visual arts, music, dance, tour management, event production, comedy, and more. The Atlanta A&E conference was Speech Thomas's brainchild. One of the reasons I am so grateful that God put that dream on his heart is that it has given all of us an opportunity to take some time to give God the glory for our gifts and talents, explore how to use them to impact the world, and discover how we can better use them to benefit the church. Since the Atlanta area is becoming the Hollywood of the South, I believe God is confirming the effort we have made during the last couple of years to reach out to all types of people and make an impact in the entertainment industry as well.

September 13 through 15, 2013 was our third conference. I can't begin to list the ways that God has produced spiritual fruit as a result of the conference, which has had an impact on believers and unbelievers alike. My prayer for every year is that those who don't see themselves as having any talent will be inspired to awaken the latent talent within. At this point, I am seeing that God himself has put his stamp of approval on the conference, and quite frankly, there's no stopping God. We look forward to the miracles he will do through the many lives that will be transformed during our time together and beyond.

Daniel and Tracy Macaluso have been great friends of Mike's and mine for over twenty years and major advocates of A&E ministries. Tracy is not only one of the most devoted disciples I know, she is also hilarious, and I love to laugh. She has been a friend through laughter and tears, and I consider her a lifer. The Macs utilize both arts and entertainment to encourage their church and reach out to their community, and their church has been fruitful as a result.

Tracy's Story

I grew up in Buffalo/Niagara Falls dancing and dreaming of being a Broadway choreographer. I married the man of my dreams—a successful rock musician. We were in pursuit of being famous; of seeing our names in lights, signing autographs, and being chased by paparazzi. But the arts and entertainment business is exactly that—a business. It's a job you have to work at really hard to pay your bills. The glamorous life is reserved for only a few.

The potential to make it big in Buffalo was very small. As a dance teacher, I frequently had students looking to me for advice and direction on life, which I was totally unequipped to give. I wanted to make a difference in the world. It was time to stop seeking praise for myself and start seeking God's applause.

So, we packed up our Chevy Nova and moved to be a part of the New York City Church of Christ's arts and entertainment ministry, working on the production of a new musical. On the second day of rehearsals, I became the choreographer working in a Broadway studio. I studied the Bible and took on the greatest role of my career—becoming a Christian! Not only had I been blessed with an amazing new life and purpose, God overwhelmingly blessed me as an artist. In the fourteen months we were in New York, I worked on ten shows.

Since moving back to Buffalo, we continue to see the impact of the A&E ministry. It has been amazing to watch our teens and youth use their talents to glorify God. They have done children's theater productions and holiday productions, singing, dancing, acting, directing, designing, choreographing, and serving. Our A&E groups have been featured in numerous concerts, festivals, and galleries. We host monthly Open Mic Nights and quarterly Performance Showcases in our community with three simple rules: no profanity, no nudity, no hate. People and cultures are coming together in a positive and spiritual way, and people are becoming Christians. People are singing praises to God. Lovin' on Buffalo blog's review concluded with, "If you are looking to get your artistic message out there and want a platform to do it on, I strongly encourage looking up BCC Arts & Entertainment. I feel so fortunate I did, and can't wait to get to another event soon!"

God has put the A&E ministry at the front of his procession in Buffalo, where it is the first impression the world encounters of God and his church. I am so grateful to be in God's playbill, using the talents he gave me to bring him a standing ovation.

Beth Brewster

My great friend Elizabeth (Beth) Brewster wears many hats: she is a wife, mom and actor. She and her husband, Jeff, have been married twenty-two years. They live in Savannah, Georgia and have two children, McKenzie (twenty) and Mark (fifteen). Beth became a Christian in the New York City daytime ministry, way back in the '80s. I have known her for about twenty years, and what I deeply respect about her is that no matter what challenges life has brought through the years, she has never stopped pursuing her dreams. Her body of work includes improv, stage, television, commercials, industrials, print work, voice-overs, and film. She has been an emcee, host, and spokesperson. She currently has two independent feature films in postproduction. The faith-based feature film Destiny Road (she plays the role of Patricia) opened in fall 2012 in Brazil to sold-out theaters and had its US premiere in Atlanta in April 2013. Elizabeth was also featured in the "Galaxy of Stars" in *The South Magazine* and in an IMDb article on "Southern Actors on the RISE!"

On top of it all, she combines all of her talent and experience and uses it to inspire women spiritually. She has written, directed, and performed her one-woman shows for several Women's Day events in cities including Atlanta, Portland, New York, Jacksonville, and Savannah.

_____ **DREAM DARE** _____

Dare to accept the talents God has given you, make the most of them, and enjoy them in the now.

For Reflection: pray...ponder...promise...practice.

Yes, we should make the most of what God gives, both the bounty and the capacity to enjoy it, accepting what's given and delighting in the work. It's God's gift! God deals out joy in the present, the now. (Ecclesiastes 5:19 MSG)

Chapter Nine

Dare to Be
a Fiercely Loved Single Woman

A woman's heart should be so hidden in God that a man has to seek Him just to find her. —Maya Angelou

An unmarried woman or virgin is concerned about the Lord's affairs: Her aim is to be devoted to the Lord in both body and spirit. (1 Corinthians 7:34b)

Undoubtedly, every woman reading this chapter who is single will have an assortment of perceptions and perspectives on her state or stage of singlehood. Plenty of single women are in their early twenties just discovering who they are, while for others, broaching the topic of singlehood is like opening a can of worms, because they may be getting pressure to marry from home, church, family, and friends. Others may be starting to feel some sort of way about always being the bridesmaid and never the bride. Women in their thirties and forties might be starting to feel hopeless as they hear their biological clocks go tick-tock, tick-tock. Those finding themselves newly single in their fifties, sixties, and later in life may perhaps be trying to figure it out all over again. Still others may possibly struggle with finding available godly men to date. Certain women endure deep pain and desperation during this time, but it is also important to state here that not every single woman desires to be married. There are the minority who don't really have a deep yearning for marriage or children at their particular phase of life.

Even though no two women are the same, I believe it's safe to say that one of the biggest dreams most women grow up cherishing is the dream to meet and marry Mr. Right by a certain time and live happily ever after. As time races by and a woman realizes that this dream or the timing of this dream may not be unfolding as she had planned, it can be excruciatingly painful and a devastating disappointment. I admire and respect my dear sisters who have been receptive to letting God take that particular dream and reshape it, and I sincerely hope the things I share won't come across as insensitive, oversimplified, or as though I am making light of your situation at all.

Over the last twenty-three years, God has placed extraordinary unmarried sisters in my life and on my heart in a significant way. I have this profound yearning for every one of God's chosen princesses to be fortified in heart and soul, beloved, and inspired to LIVE and be her best for her King Jesus.

Additionally, single people often postpone life and happiness. They say, "When I get married, then I'll be happy" or "When I have children, then I'll be happy" or "When I have a comfortable home and a comfortable salary, *then* I'll be happy." My genuine intention is to spur you on to unbridle your dreams as you wait on God to provide the suitable mate or the ideal situation for you.

Hence, how would you describe what you think and how you feel about your stage in life? How we think about God and ourselves is of the utmost importance. Proverbs 23:7 (AMP) says, *"for as he thinks in his heart, so is he."* How we see ourselves (I'm worthless; no one would ever be interested in me; God has forgotten me) is what we become, and how you see this stage of life (being single stinks) will be what it becomes. Let's put it this way: you exude what you conclude. What you think in your heart seeps through your pores and speaks volumes to those around you. So let's challenge some of the stinking thinking and prevent it from taking up residence in your mind.

Myth #1: Being single is a curse. Something must be wrong with me because nobody wants me.
Truth: Single means whole, complete, separate, and unique. You can't be loved more than you are right now.

Remember Eve, the first woman and wife and the mother of all living. When God built the woman, she was not half a person; she was another whole; she was complete before the marriage to Adam. The two became spiritually and in every way united (Genesis 2:24). Some have understood this as two halves becoming one whole, implying that when you are single, you are not a whole person. This is simply not true.

To continue, from God's perspective, you can't be loved more than you are at this moment. He does not love you less because you are single! God gave his *one and only* to show the extent of his love for you and me. I am completely convinced somebody loves me when that person sacrifices for me. Christ sacrificed it all for me. The devil is a liar and the father of lies, and one of the biggest lies he tells single women is that no one wants them, when in fact the most important Person in the universe gave his all just so you could be his very own. He is your *Abba* (daddy), your Father, and he loves you!

Actually, women tend to see God the way they saw their earthly fathers, and unfortunately, many of us did not grow up with our dads. For others, the example we did grow up with was a poor reflection of our heavenly Father.

Through the years, I have watched the special relationship grow between my daughter Alexis (now twenty) and her daddy. Of course, her daddy is not perfect, and both Mom and Dad have made a multitude of mistakes along the way, but regardless of all the imperfections, the confidence she has in her father's love and the love she has for him have shaped her life.

Let's Treasure Our Heavenly Father
Your Father:

- Is your Creator, who made you and formed you (Deuteronomy 32:6)
- Is your Abba, your Father (Romans 8:15)
- Makes us heirs of God and co-heirs with Christ (Romans 8:17)
- Is abounding in love (Psalm 103:8)
- Cares for and has compassion for his children (Psalm 103)
- Is a father to the fatherless, a defender of widows (Psalm 68:5)
- Is your God, the Rock your Savior (Psalm 89:26)
- Understands (Psalm 103:14)
- Is the potter; we are all the work of his hands (Isaiah 64:8)
- Already knows your needs and will give you everything you need (Matthew 6:8, 31–33)
- Does not play favorites (Matthew 12:50)
- Satisfies your desires with good things (Psalm 103:5)
- Answers when you ask (Luke 11:9)
- Wants you with him forever (John 14:2–4)

The truth is, on this earth we may never have all of life's answers that we would like to have, as the apostle Paul indicates in 1 Corinthians 13:12. Even still, we can be secure in his inseparable love and desire for us. Joyce Meyer, in her book, *Straight Talk on Loneliness,* states, "Proverbs 3:5, 6 tells us that trust in the Lord brings assurance and direction: Lean on, trust in, and be confident in the Lord with all your heart and mind and do not rely on your own insight or understanding. In all your ways know, recognize, and acknowledge Him, and He will direct and make straight and plain your paths. When we face a time of crisis in life, we need direction. These scriptures tell us that trusting God is the way to find that direction. Trust requires allowing some unanswered questions to be in your life!"[1] This truth is hard for us to deal with, because human nature wants to understand everything.

> **Myth #2:** Marriage is the cure for my loneliness.
> **Truth:** Loneliness in itself is a form of grief; it is not a sin, so don't beat yourself up and walk around feeling guilty for having lonely feelings.

According to *Webster's Dictionary,* words like "lonely" and "lonesome" convey a sense of isolation felt as a result of a lack of companionship. Meyer asks, "Are you alone (independent, solitary, on your own)? Or, are you lonely (desolate, deserted, dejected due to a lack of companionship)? There is a very real difference. It's important to realize that just because you are alone, it doesn't mean you must be lonely or lonesome." She adds that even being in companionship with other people is not a guaranteed cure for loneliness and that the conditions that create loneliness are sometimes temporary situations.[2] I remember when we first moved to Atlanta and a best friend I had here had just moved to New York. I was in a new home, in a new town, having a new experience, and I felt a temporary feeling of loneliness, but I eventually made new friends. But then, there are the situations that create a permanent sense of loneliness.

The hard-to-face fact is that loneliness is an inevitable part of life. Even Jesus in the flesh felt lonely at times, and he was the most well-adjusted person who ever lived. Yet he knew times of abandonment.

Most likely, loneliness will visit all of us at one time or another in our lives. It often knocks on the door of the shy or extremely timid; it sits down for coffee with those who feel misunderstood and those in leadership. It tries to make its home with the divorced and unmarried; the widowed; the elderly; those who feel rejected; those who feel "odd" or different from other people; the abused; those unable to maintain healthy relationships, especially with the opposite sex; those who relocate or change employment—and the list goes on and on.[3]

Incidentally, marriage doesn't ensure an end to loneliness. There are millions of married people who are lonely too, still looking for the fulfillment that they are not getting from their spouse.

Let me just say this right here: 2 Corinthians 6:14 is in the Bible for a reason. *"Do not be yoked together with unbelievers. For what do righteousness and wickedness have in common? Or what fellowship can light have with darkness?"* It is not a suggestion or a disputable matter; it is a "Do not." It reminds me of what a good parent says to instruct their children and keep them safe: "Do not open the door when an adult is not home." "Do not put your hand on the stove!" The words "do not" can be two of the most loving, lifesaving words we can hear or say.

If you have been a faithful believer in Christ and now you are tempted to date or marry someone who is not, *"Do not."* Being unequally yoked is about to cause you more pain and suffering then you realize. There are fatal effects of neglecting Scripture, and you don't want to start off a marriage on a fatal foundation.

What is a fatal foundation? Building a house on sand.

"Therefore everyone who hears these words of mine and puts them into practice is like a wise man who built his house on the rock. The rain came down, the streams rose, and the winds blew and beat against that house; yet it did not fall, because it had its foundation on the rock. But everyone who hears these words of mine and does not put them into practice is like a foolish man who built his house on sand. The rain came down, the streams rose, and the winds blew and beat against that house, and it fell with a great crash." (Matthew 7:24-28)

The unbeliever you are tempted to be yoked with can be a great guy, have a nice personality, do good deeds, and even attend a church. He can be the most handsome man you've laid eyes on and a good provider. Who can blame you for compromising, right?

Honestly, when you have already given your heart away to an unbeliever and are at the point of thinking it's ok to compromise, you are in deep. I know; I have been there as a younger Christian. It took God to break the trancelike state I was in. It took this prayer: "God, you know I love you, and bottom line, I want to end up with you for all eternity. If this situation will not lead me to heaven, give me the strength to cut it off." It was cut off the day after the prayer. It took accepting the sobering fact that, if this man does not have a solid foundation on Christ and in his word, he is like the foolish man who built his house on the sand. Or to conspicuously illustrate the point, he is like the foolish man who builds your house on the sand. It took me saying to myself, "Why am I falling for a guy who hasn't fallen for my God? How prideful of me: I like the way he treats me, but I could care less about how he treats my God! Uh-oh!" When I came to my senses, that was a deal breaker.

If you choose to take your life into your own hands, you should expect distress, as Deuteronomy 22:10 warns us: *"Do not plow with an ox and a donkey yoked together"* Why? The weaker partner will be hurt. Amos 3:3 (NLT) says, *"Can two people walk together without agreeing on the direction?"* We all know the answer is a resounding "No!" Just know that you are signing up for confusion, complication, and chaos. And PLEASE don't risk your relationship with God because "I see all my friends do it and they seem happy." Remember this promise that God has made to you:

> *Do not let your heart envy sinners,*
> > *but always be zealous for the fear of the LORD.*
> *There is surely a future hope for you,*
> > *and your hope will not be cut off.* (Proverbs 23:17–18)

If you accept the truth that loneliness is unavoidable, what can you do about it? Jesus' solution for loneliness was choosing friends to share his life with and spend time with, being immersed with meeting the needs of others, and constantly offering up prayers and petitions with fervent cries and tears to the one who could save him (Hebrews 5:7).

I just want to emphasize here how much we need friends. Simply put, Jesus who was God in the flesh, chose the twelve apostles to come and be with him as companions, not because they were like him, not because they were supertalented, and not because they were giants of faithfulness. They weren't any of those things. The *NIV Life Application Bible* makes the point that he chose them *to be with him* and to be sent out because they were willing. At a time when his soul was overwhelmed with sorrow to the point of death, he needed his friends (Matthew 26:38). How much more do we need ours? Don't sit on the sidelines watching everybody enjoy their relationships. Imitate Jesus, pray about it, initiate with someone who is willing, and spend time with them. Friendships are food for the soul.

> **Myth #3:** You are less valuable in God's church if you are unmarried.
> **Truth:** You are an indispensable part of the body of Christ.

The Bible regards marriage as a sacred and holy relationship reflecting the relationship of Christ and the church. As a married woman, I am truly humbled and honored to have the amazing privilege and to enjoy the benefits of the marriage relationship, which displays the oneness of Jesus and his bride. So please hear me when I say that the last thing I want to do is to take away from this glorious spiritual union, because it is such a special, important thing, especially these days when we face a rising antimarriage culture. I just think sometimes we view marriage as reaching the Promised Land, the be-all and end-all, the most important calling, and we think that if you are not married something must be wrong with you. I have known women to carry around the feeling of somehow being less or even to feel like their singlehood was a crippling, contagious disease that nobody wanted to catch—and that makes me very sad, mainly because I don't think this is Jesus' heart on the matter.

The Bible clearly states that in Christ Jesus we are all children of God through faith, and that in his eyes, our age, race, and social status do not change the fact that we belong to him and are a part of God's body (Galatians 3:26–28). The ground is level at the foot of the cross where we all stand. As 1 Corinthians 12 tells us, the type of ministry God blesses us with may vary, but we are all members of one body.[4]

> **Myth #4:** I will die if I don't have sex.
> **Truth:** The biggest sexual organ is the brain.

Have you ever wondered how Jesus dealt with his sexual needs and knowing marriage wasn't in the cards for him? He was tempted with everything we are tempted with, yet did not sin. Paul was celibate and, yes, it was his gift (1 Corinthians 7:7–8), but my point is that he lived a full and healthy life being celibate.

I'm not saying it's always easy to be celibate. That's why the Bible says we must learn to control our bodies in a way that is honorable (1 Thessalonians 4:4). I am saying that God would not have you in an impossible situation, with no plan to work in you. Look at all the examples in Jesus' life.

Also, *eros* love (erotic love, a strong feeling, a sense of falling in love, based upon a circumstance) without *agape* love (unconditional, based upon a decision and a commitment) is not the greatest form of love you can experience. According to Mark 12:30–31 (KJV),

> *"And thou shalt love the Lord thy God with all thy heart, and with all thy soul, and with all thy mind, and with all thy strength: this is the first commandment.*
>
> *"And the second is like, namely this, Thou shalt love thy neighbor as thyself. There is none other commandment greater than these."*

Myth #5: I can never be content unless my circumstances change.
Truth: We all have to learn the secret of being content or we can never be happy.

I believe that Philippians 4:4–9 gives us the keys to contentment and that Jesus is the perfect example.

> *Rejoice in the Lord always. I will say it again: Rejoice! Let your gentleness be evident to all. The Lord is near. Do not be anxious about anything, but in every situation, by prayer and petition, with thanksgiving, present your requests to God. And the peace of God, which transcends all understanding, will guard your hearts and your minds in Christ Jesus.*
>
> *Finally, brothers and sisters, whatever is true, whatever is noble, whatever is right, whatever is pure, whatever is lovely, whatever is admirable—if anything is excellent or praiseworthy—think about such things. Whatever you have learned or received or heard from me, or seen in me— put it into practice. And the God of peace will be with you.*

We rejoice in the Lord, not necessarily in the circumstance. We rejoice in the fact that no matter what circumstance, he is with us and is able to supply all things at all times, giving us all that we need. Jesus is such a stellar example of this because he left a perfect God and the perfect situation in heaven to live in bodily form among sinful humans. Even though he must have longed to be back in heaven with God, he was able to be content here on earth.

We are not to be anxious about anything (ouch). Anxiety does absolutely nothing to change a situation. It's a waste of time, but praying about everything makes all the difference. Prayer leads us to an unfathomable peace, which is a safeguard for our hearts and minds. Also, thinking with a godly perspective on life (whatever is true, pure, lovely, admirable, and so on) helps us to be grateful for what we do have and more willing to accept a situation for the time being.

Ultimately, being content does not mean we love our circumstances and hope they never go away. Jesus even prayed in the Garden of Gethsemane three times, starting with, *"If it is possible, may this cup be taken from me. Yet not as I will but as you will"* and concluding with, *"If it is not possible for this cup to be taken away unless I drink it, may your will be done"* (Matthew 26:39, 42).

We can hope, we can plan, and we can pray that our circumstances will change, but the bottom line is that either God designed these circumstances for your good or allowed you to have these circumstances, right now, for your good. We might as well be faithful and flexible and allow him to fulfill our dreams or change them as he sees fit.[5] In the meantime, do not put your dreams on hold and be stuck in the mud of discontentment.

Myth #6: It's a hopeless situation.
Truth: Nothing is hopeless for God. Wait, hope for, and expect.

We know that hope deferred makes the heart sick (Proverbs 13:12a); therefore it's imperative to remain hopeful in your situation. Wait, hope and expect instead of living a life of worry and regret. "Hope is the oxygen of the soul."[6] David wrote in Psalm 27:13–14 (AMP),

> *[What, what would have become of me] had I not believed that I would see the Lord's goodness in the land of the living!*
>
> *Wait and hope for and expect the Lord; be brave and of good courage and let your heart be stout and enduring. Yes, wait for and hope for and expect the Lord.*

My friend, what will become of you if you stop believing in God's goodness? Wait for, hope for, and expect the Lord.

I had the honor of meeting my dear friend Jacqueline when we first moved to Georgia. Since I have known her, she has greatly desired to be found by the right man and to marry. As the years have gone by, I have watched her struggle and grow stronger, pray and find peace, and cry and cling to God's word. Through it all, she has not stopped giving to the single women around her, helping countless women with their relationship with God. She is being refined through it all as she chooses every day to put her trust in God. She has surrendered to the fact that her timing has not been

God's timing, but she still faithfully holds on to her dream to one day be married.

Below is a draft from her upcoming book.

Jacqueline's Story

My book is a culmination of the personal struggles that I have gone through in my walk of celibacy and singlehood. When I studied the Bible during my conversion almost seventeen years ago, I gave little thought to the idea of singlehood and being celibate. I didn't consider the full ramifications of what it truly means to live purely. At that time, I was lost and going to hell, and all that mattered to me was that I get right with God. During much of the past seventeen years, what I gave little thought to has become a source of great pain, struggle, and grief. I have had to struggle on my knees in prayer and with much Bible study throughout my Christian walk to get to a place of peace and contentment with my lot of singlehood. Celibacy and purity is more than not having sex before marriage. It's about Jesus being Lord in every area of your life and he being your source of fulfillment.

For years, I beat my head against a wall because I could not understand why God had not chosen to bless me with a husband. I constantly heard from friends and family, "Jacqueline, I just don't understand why you're not married. You're such a pretty girl and you have so much going for you." The whole time while they were saying this, their faces would be fixed in an expression of pity and perplexity. For years, I lived in a place of not understanding why I was still single, which ultimately led to despair, hopelessness, bitterness, and resentment toward God for not doing anything about it. To add to that, I've seen my closest friends, sisters from all over the kingdom who were my heroes in the faith, decide one by one to turn away from the path of celibacy and leave the church and God because they could endure no longer the pain of being single.

I have had to spend much time soul-searching and studying the Scriptures. Finally, God brought relief and freedom through the message of the cross. A few years ago, for the first time in my Christian walk, the message and love of the cross became personal, crystal clear, and very real to me. Experiencing the love of the cross has torn off the chains of the mental and emotional baggage that I had been carrying for so long and that had manifested itself in my obsession for marriage. It has taken me almost seventeen years to reach a place of surrender in my walk of celibacy, but I can testify that time always proves God's faithfulness. I don't come before you as a woman who doesn't struggle with being single any more or who has abandoned the desire for marriage. My dream is still to get married and have a family. I come before you as one who is slowly realizing that the key to contentment in the midst of waiting on the Lord is surrender. Surrender, no matter our situation and circumstance, is easy to say but challenging to live daily, yet with it comes a peace and hope that leaves one with an ability to still dare to dream despite the challenges.

When the arrows of insecurity, loneliness, and faithlessness start to attack, I now know how to handle it and overcome. Now I understand why God has allowed me to be single for all these years. I believe singlehood and celibacy have refined my character like nothing else has. Nothing has driven me to my knees more and has so taught me the true meaning of perseverance and endurance. Singlehood has forced me to look deep inside and deal with my past and to take my faith to a higher level, learning what it means to walk by faith and not by sight. I now have a story to share with you that I hope will inspire and encourage you to experience and live successfully the life of celibacy. I hope that what I have learned will help you to be your best for God. To God be the glory! For the joy set before me, I endure.

_____ DREAM DARE _____

Dare to live like you are God's princess who is chosen, royal, set apart, and special.

For Reflection: pray…ponder…promise…practice.

But you are a chosen people, a royal priesthood, a holy nation, God's special possession, that you may declare the praises of him who called you out of darkness into his wonderful light. (1 Peter 2:9)

Chapter Ten

Dare to Be a Single Mother Who Relies on God

Faith makes things possible, not easy. —Author unknown

This chapter is dedicated to the many single mothers whom I have had the pleasure of knowing, serving with, and loving through the years. Whether they came to be single mothers by divorce, the death of a husband, or having children out of wedlock, the bottom line is that they have had or now have the daunting task of raising children as the only parent in the household. Most of us would agree that although parenting is a blessing, it is also very demanding even for two parents. According to the U.S. Census Bureau, there are 10 million single mothers raising children in the united states and 27 million children living in father-absent homes.[1]

I could not write this chapter without expressing my admiration, respect, and love for the single moms whom Mike and I served in the Bronx and Harlem ministries. Those mighty women became some of the most faithful disciples we have had the privilege of knowing. They were overflowing with gratitude for God and his church, dedicated to their children, and some of the most fruitful disciples in the church. They traveled via bus and train through the rain or snow with children in tow, without excuse or complaint. They were *happy!* They will forever bring joy to my heart whenever I think of them, the Warrior Women who called us all higher and taught us what sacrifice really meant.

A few years ago, I spent some time in the Bible with Hagar and her son, and by the end of my study of her life, I was in tears and overwhelmed with gratitude for God's goodness shown to her. It touched my heart so and I was so excited about what I saw in God's character, heart, and provision that I literally wanted to tell the world, especially all the women who are out there every day striving to love, nurture, train, and raise up their children. It's so exciting to me that I get to do exactly that right now in writing this chapter.

Single moms, there is HOPE! You can't change what was, but you can influence what will be. You can't change others, but you can change you with God's help. If God made a way in the wilderness for this single woman and her son without friends, family, or resources to help her, he will surely make a way for the single moms of today,[2] especially for those who have surrendered to his leadership of their lives.

Hagar was an Egyptian slave of Sarai, the first wife of Abram. She probably had served Sarai for at least the ten years since Abram's household had come out of Egypt. Because Sarai had been barren for so long and her husband Abram was getting older, Sarai came up with the idea to help God fulfill his promise (Genesis 16:1–3). You can already tell this is going to be a spiritual disaster, right? She offered Hagar to Abram as a second wife (Genesis 16:3). Sarai struggled with something we women tend to struggle with: control. She just had to take things into her own hands to fix the situation. She wanted something bad, and if God was not going to come through, she would make it happen. Can you relate? I can. I've gotten tired of waiting on God and taken things into my own hands, and I have paid the price.

> *When she knew she was pregnant, she began to despise her mistress. Then Sarai said to Abram, "You are responsible for the wrong I am suffering. I put my slave in your arms, and now that she knows she is pregnant, she despises me. May the LORD judge between you and me."*
> *"Your slave is in your hands," Abram said. "Do with her whatever you think best." Then Sarai mistreated Hagar; so she fled from her.*
> (Genesis 16:4–6)

Have you noticed that when we don't do things God's way and sometimes even when we do, life can be pretty messy? All three parties were involved in this sinful situation, which would cause bitter pain and suffering that would last to this day. Sarai in her unbelief and impatience distrusted God, and instead of Abram saying no, maybe his lust and definitely his lack of trust took over and he agreed. Because Hagar was a slave, the situation was out of her control, but it wasn't all bad at first. Carrying Abram's child brought her honor. There must have been a lot going on in her heart.

"When she knew she was pregnant, she began to despise her mistress." Women, can you just imagine what it must have been like living in that household? The evil looks, snide remarks, and taunts—it got so bad, Sarai then blamed Abram for everything and mistreated Hagar harshly, making her life a living hell. The situation got so unbearable that Hagar chose to escape into the desert with nothing and no one to depend on, pregnant, all alone, and afraid.

I have never been a single mother, so I can only imagine that many single moms have felt at one time or another exactly the way Hagar must have. Dealing with a situation like this one, which is far from ideal, can be emotionally and mentally disturbing, physically draining, socially degrading, and spiritually challenging. How was she to provide for her child in the desert with no resources? Oh, my Lord!

> *The angel of the LORD found Hagar near a spring in the desert; it was the spring that is beside the road to Shur. And he said, "Hagar, slave of Sarai, where have you come from, and where are you going?"*
>
> *"I'm running away from my mistress Sarai," she answered.*
>
> *Then the angel of the LORD told her, "Go back to your mistress and submit to her." The angel added, "I will increase your descendants so much that they will be too numerous to count."*
>
> *The angel of the LORD also said to her:*
>
> > *"You are now pregnant*
> > *and you will give birth to a son.*
> > *You shall name him Ishmael,*
> > *for the LORD has heard of your misery.*
> > *He will be a wild donkey of a man;*
> > *his hand will be against everyone*
> > *and everyone's hand against him,*
> > *and he will live in hostility*
> > *toward all his brothers."*
>
> *She gave this name to the LORD who spoke to her: "You are the God who sees me," for she said, "I have now seen the One who sees me." That is why the well was called Beer Lahai Roi; it is still there, between Kadesh and Bered.*
>
> *So Hagar bore Abram a son, and Abram gave the name Ishmael to the son she had borne.* (Genesis 16:7–15)

This scene is astounding! Here we have Hagar, a poor slave, a no-body, who was being treated as though she was worthless, in the desert alone. But was she really alone? Absolutely not. The angel was in hot pursuit of her. He obviously already knew who she was but asked her where she had come from and where she was going. I don't think that was just a random question. I think that's what God does; he wants us to listen, think, and then choose to follow his direction, and that's what Hagar did. She did not argue. She obeyed when the angel said, *"Go back to your mistress and submit to her."* It was illegal for a slave to flee, and even in her suffering God expected her to do what was right.[3] So convicting! It must have been exhilarating to have a personal revelation from God himself and a promise for her future! *"You will give birth to a son. You shall name him Ishmael."* Ishmael means "God hears."[4] This woman and her son's life were so important to God that he personally intervened on her behalf, gave her lifesaving direction, and spoke words of comfort and promise to her. This should remind us all that nothing and no-body goes unnoticed to God. He sees, cares and acts. He is always at work, especially when we are weak and in difficult situations. In fact, 2 Corinthians 12:9–10 shows us that God's grace is sufficient for us and his power is made perfect in weakness.

What a magnificent encounter between God and this woman. She was so inspired she gave this name to the Lord who spoke to her: *"You are the God who sees me,"* because she had now seen the one who was watching over her.

It moves my heart to know that when we are in the desert of pain and suffering, near the spring beside the road of desperation, running away from our misery, God is hot on our heels. He meets us where we are, enlightens us, kindles our souls, and reminds us of his promise. He sees you and he sees me. God had a bigger dream for Hagar and her son than anyone could have imagined, and he had a plan for her deliverance.

Then God kept his promise to Abram, and Isaac was born to nine-ty-year-old Sarah. Hagar would find herself and her son forced away this time, after Sarah found Hagar's teenage son mocking Isaac. Obviously, the relationship between Hagar and Sarah had worsened and had affected the relationship between the boys. This time Sarah demanded that Abraham send Hagar and her son away, but wait…before you get an attitude with Abraham, you should know that he was greatly distressed so he sought the advice of God. Yahweh told Abraham not to be troubled but to do as his wife demanded, because not only would Isaac carry the Abrahamic line, but a nation would come from the line of Ishmael as well (Genesis 21:9–13).

Don't you feel much better about Abraham now? He was concerned for his son, so he prayed.

Early the next morning, Abraham gathered Hagar and Ishmael and released Hagar and her son from being slaves of their household. He packed them up and sent them off with some food and a skin of water for a journey into the wilderness of Beersheba. Hagar and her son wandered aimlessly until the skin of water was completely dried up. I can't help but be a little ticked with Abraham for sending this meager "child support" but not really taking care of his responsibility. Ladies, do you have anyone in your life like that? I am comforted to know that even when man falls short of his responsibility, God's got it. Just keep reading.

I don't know if you can relate to feeling like you are in the wilderness wrestling with the feelings of fear, anger, betrayal, and hopelessness. What happens next has got to be one of the most painful things for any mother to experience. Hagar was in an insuperable situation and literally had to watch her son dying of thirst. Broken to pieces and crushed, Hagar put her boy under one of the bushes and sat down opposite him because she was not able to endure watching him die, and there was absolutely nothing she could do to save him, as she was dying as well. And as she sat there, she began to sob.

This next part is extraordinary. God heard the boy's voice and sent an angel to confirm to Hagar that her son would become a great nation. Miraculously, a well of water then appeared and saved their lives. Did you hear that, ladies? God provided a well in the wilderness, saved their lives, and made a stupendous promise. The son of Hagar would be a great nation.

Nothing, and I mean nothing, can stop God from acting. When he has a plan for your life, *"there is no wisdom, no insight, no plan that can succeed against the Lord"* Proverbs 21:30.

I have fallen in love with Hagar. Although to me her situation seemed unbearable and she had even given up, God made a way for her and her son when she had no friends, no family, and no resources. He had seen, he had heard, and he was faithful. She is a sign of hope to all women when we are at our weakest and all alone. God says, *"Do not be afraid"* (Genesis 21:17).

As a single mother, you may feel all the feelings we touched on in this chapter and more besides. I hope you have been encouraged and reminded that God will always be there taking care of you and your child if you let him. There is a bigger picture. Who knows? You might be raising the next Barack Obama, Bill Cosby, Julia Roberts, Angel Maldonado, Teregi Coleman, Manuel Rivera, Ayanna Stevens, Amarillis Mercado, Frank Davis, or Olga Bird.

Mike and I met Olga after Mike became close friends with her son Angel. When I met her, I was drawn to her from that first meeting. Her joy, giving spirit, and zeal for God was and is contagious. I consider it a complete honor to be one of the women who opened the scriptures with her and helped her on her journey to become a Christian.

Olga's Story

I was born in Puerto Rico on Valentine's Day, but unfortunately, finding love would be a lifelong quest for me. My mom was a drug addict and her mom an alcoholic, so when I was three months old, my mom gave me away to a family friend. My father was unknown.

The family I grew up with had their own issues. They made sure to let me know that I did not belong to them and that one day my mom would come and pick me up. There was not much affection except from one the oldest siblings, whom I named my Tata. She always took me to church and loved me as if I were hers, and from that time I remember always talking to God like my best friend.

At seven years old, I was already feeling anxious and as though I didn't belong to anyone. I remember my mom came back to get me, but instead of feeling excited to go with her, I hid in a church so she couldn't take me away.

As a young teenager, the feeling of being different and all alone persisted. I really believed I had no future. At seventeen, looking for love, I started dating my first husband and was married by the age of eighteen. By the time I was twenty-one, I found myself with two children and an unfaithful husband who used drugs and alcohol. I was so hurt and alone, I would always ask myself, "Where is God?" Eventually I decided to get a divorce.

Although I loved being a mother and I loved my kids, it wouldn't take long to find out how hard it was to be a single mom. At least I had the security of knowing my kids were with me, and I promised myself I would fight for their happiness and never leave them.

While I was hard at work, striving to provide for my kids and still hoping for love, I met a man who was thirteen years older than I. At the time, I thought he was perfect for me. He treated the kids really well, was a professional, had money, helped me pay the bills, and made sure to tell me the things I wanted to hear.

The first week I moved in with him, he came home and found me talking with a neighbor. He called me into the bathroom and hit me so hard I ended up on the floor, full of bruises and with my heart crushed. On that day, I thought he had broken my spirit and taken my soul. I asked myself, "What happened?" He was a super nice guy who suddenly turned into a beast. For the next few years, I suffered from his controlling nature and from physical and mental abuse. If I made any kind of mistake, I would surely pay for it.

When we moved to Florida, he promised me that life would be different because it was the environment in Puerto Rico that made him behave the way he did. We bought a house and got married, and the first year in Florida it seemed like things were going to be okay, until one day I opened a bank account and they made a mistake by putting my name first instead of his. He became so enraged, he broke my nose. At this point in my life, I started having panic attacks and was scared of everything.

I tried to leave him a few times, but I struggled with where I would go and who would help me. Again, I thought my kids deserved better, even if I had to sacrifice. When I started going to church, I got the courage to get on my knees and pray to God asking him to remove this man from my life, even if I had to pay the price of losing everything, because he was affecting my relationship with God. A week later, I found out I was pregnant. A week after that, he left me, pregnant with two children in Florida. I had no family, friends, or job and I didn't speak English.

That part of my life was very hard and reminds me of Isaiah 57:15 because although I was alone and broke again and almost lost my baby, all of this prompted me to search for God more intensely. I knew he was close to me, watching out for my children, opening doors, and using people to guide me. God gave me another gift from him, a baby boy. I named him Gabriel like the angel warrior. He gave me strength to keep fighting. I am so thankful for my church at the time. They helped me through life once again, and they also helped me build a faith in God, although I did not understand how God wanted me to live as a Christian. The great thing was that I always read my Bible, prayed, and went to church. I also knew something was missing in my spiritual life. I had questions about God, my faith, and the church.

After another disappointing and very nasty divorce, I was left with nothing. I struggled to work hard as a waitress, also cleaning houses, babysitting, and working two jobs. I went from one relationship to another, from one loser to another with the hope of having my heart's desire (Psalm 37:4). All I wanted was a home with a faithful, decent, responsible husband who would be a good father to my sons.

At the age of thirty-four, I started having headaches and found out my brain was bleeding. Stress was killing me. My vein stopped bleeding, and I believe God healed me. One more time, God was there listening and comforting me. I asked God to let me live to raise my kids, and this time I would not settle for less than what God had for me. I was going to change my ways.

Although we were a "dysfunctional family," I always felt that we weren't. Excluding the men, we were a happy family, close and loving. My boys were my priority. I always told them the truth, even when it was hard for them to understand. Angel, my oldest one, was my close friend and the man of the house. He started hanging out with friends and using marihuana, but I didn't believe it because he was so smart and very mature for his age, and his grades were amazing. Javier was my helper and caregiver and always making sure that everything was in order. Gaby was our baby. I decided to live the rest of my life for them and for God and to make myself a better person. I went to school and became a real estate salesperson. I lived a peaceful life without a man. God taught me to find love in him and him only (Isaiah 62:3–5). I surrendered all.

Soon after finding my first love, Jesus, I met the love of my life, my son's wrestling coach. He was the man I always dreamed of. My life changed radically for good, but I still felt something missing spiritually. We joined a denominational church, and I was extremely active in the Spanish ministry for abused women. I enjoyed serving them and found great purpose in doing so, but when Angel went to college, got in trouble, and then found Jesus, I watched his life change completely. Through him I began to see what it meant to really live with a spiritual purpose and what it meant to be a real disciple of Jesus. Because I thought I was safe being the "Christian" I was, even though I could see the difference between my life and Angel's, it would take eight years of watching his and his wife's lifestyle, his church, and the testimonies of the saints. These things "preached" to me (1 Timothy 4:16) until I surrendered and decided to study the Bible and make Jesus my Lord. God forgave me and gave me a new life. Jeremiah 29:11 showed me that God had great plans to prosper me and not to harm me, and glory be to God, it is true. My life is a testimony of this. I learned not to stop dreaming and not to lose hope.

Today, God has done more than I could have asked for or imagined. My son Angel graduated from Florida State University and is the lead evangelist of the GACC. His wife, Christina, is serving alongside him and is a sister and daughter to me. He couldn't ask for a better wife. Angel is tenderhearted and a lovable father to Layla, my first granddaughter. He's a successful man of God. I call him the "Chosen One." And Angel is still my best friend.

My son Javier graduated from Chattanooga University. He's a teacher and coach. He's married to Amanda, an awesome woman with many talents. I am so grateful to have her as a daughter. My son has high values, and the seed of Jesus that I planted in his heart is flourishing. I call him "Javi My Heart."

My son Gaby was baptized a year ago. I had the honor of baptizing him. He's studying to become a nurse at Shorter University in Georgia. His faith and convictions are growing daily. I could not be more blessed than to have such a giving and responsible son. I call him "Gaby My Baby Boy." He will always be my baby.

My husband is a dedicated wrestling coach, husband and father. He walks with integrity and wisdom. His faith is growing, as I am the Bible he reads. It is evident that God is working in his life. As a wrestling coach, he has had an opportunity to touch many lives, especially a teenager named Olmo. He and his wife, Vanity, and their children are part of our family. They both became disciples.

My Tata and best friend, Alice, Yanitza my spiritual daughter, and Marie her fourteen-year-old daughter are now disciples too. We are working together as sisters and partners in the faith.

Now I see that God's dream for my life was to experience the greatest love of all, with no broken spirit and no taken soul. God's plan was never to harm me. My choices, lack of guidance, and disobedience brought consequences that led me to Christ. Although the enemy tried to destroy me, our great God, through the blood of Jesus, saved me!

_____ DREAM DARE _____

Dare to ask God for an undivided heart.

For Reflection: pray...ponder...promise...practice.

Teach me your way, LORD,
*   that I may rely on your faithfulness;*
give me an undivided heart,
*   that I may fear your name.* (Psalm 86:11)

Chapter Eleven

Dare to More Than Conquer

A woman is like a tea bag: you never know how strong she is until you put her in hot water. —Nancy Reagan

No, in all these things we are more than conquerors through him who loved us. For I am convinced that neither death nor life, neither angels nor demons, neither the present nor the future, nor any powers, neither height nor depth, nor anything else in all creation, will be able to separate us from the love of God that is in Christ Jesus our Lord. (Romans 8:37–39)

Certainly most folks who are truly living in Christ would say that Romans 8:37–39 contains one of the most reassuring promises in God's word. Even those who don't claim to be Christians would agree that it is an inspiring promise. For those of us who have been chosen by God and who choose God, we can enjoy great comfort in knowing there is no trouble, no hardship, no persecution, no famine—absolutely nothing—that can separate us from the loving favor of our triumphant Christ.

Yes, for Christians, right in the middle of all the impossibilities, unlikelihoods and impracticalities of life, we are already more than spiritual conquers. Actually, due to God's grace, we have already been made partakers in the most powerful, immense, everlasting victory of all victories that Christ brought to completion by his death, burial and resurrection. It is the ultimate statement of security. Our victorious position in Christ is not based on our situation; it's based on our salvation. It's not based on religion; it's based on our relationship with him. We are united by faith to the victorious one, the Lord Jesus Christ!

Given that he is victorious, our victory does not rest on our strength, knowledge, or pride. We won't always feel victorious or look victorious. Being more than a conquer does not mean we don't face daily burdens, stress, demands, injustices, and troubles. It doesn't mean we won't struggle with temptations and addictions. It simply means what 1 Corinthians 15:57 (NASB) says: *"But thanks be to God, who gives us the victory through our Lord Jesus Christ."*

Mike and I were blessed to meet Will and Rose Ashley in the early '90s. Mike and several of the brothers were sharing the life-changing word of God with Will, and it didn't take long for him to become a Christian. I'll never forget the night Will brought Rose to dinner so all of us could meet. She was very direct and spunky and I liked her from the start. I remember thinking, "This is one tough lady," and soon after, we would witness the miracles God would do with her tender heart. When I recently asked Rose who her spiritual hero is, she said Deborah, a fearless, courageous woman of God. That did not surprise me. Rose is truly a fearless, courageous woman, and her life inspires all of God's children to claim the conqueror inside each one of us.

Rose's Story

I was born in Brooklyn the second of five siblings; I have three sisters and one brother. My mom was a typical Puerto Rican mom; she stayed home and took care of us while my dad worked hard as a bellboy at the Royal Manhattan Hotel, among other things. You could say he was a hustler and did what he had to do to take care of us. I loved my dad a great deal, but growing up I did not have the close relationship I would have liked to have with him. He focused a great deal on my older sister because not only did he want to see her do well, but he also expected her to be an example as the oldest. Then there was the sister a year behind me, who was born with muscular dystrophy along with some slight retardation.

My sister did not walk until she was seven years old, so we all had to pitch in to help with her, and many times I felt like I was being overlooked. I know that my dad felt as if he did not have to worry about me because I got good grades. I was involved in dance and I loved it and school as well. Even though I was doing all of the right things, I began to get involved with all of the wrong things while still bringing home good grades and being home on time. I think that parents can sometimes believe that because their kids are doing well in school, they are not involved in dangerous behavior.

I had my first drink at the age of eight. I remember my parents would have New Year's Eve parties and I would volunteer to clean up so I could drink whatever was left in the cups. I remember getting pretty woozy and having to go to bed. I actually liked the high, but of course, not the hangover. I began smoking at the age of nine, and by the time I was eleven, I snorted my first bag of heroin. My best friend's boyfriend sold it. Throughout high school I experimented with a few things: mescaline, marijuana, uppers, and downers; alcohol was just a norm for me.

At the age of fifteen, I became a Jehovah's Witness and remained one pretty much throughout high school. You could say it kept me out of some trouble for a little while, even though there was a group of us who would drink and party together. I remember one day inviting over one of the young men I liked. We went downstairs to the basement and began drinking. My mom and dad were both upstairs and trusted that I was doing the right thing because I was a Witness and at one time was very serious about my faith. I'm not quite sure if he brought wine with him to the house or whether there was some already in the house, being that it was a finished basement, but we both got drunk and unpleasant things happened.

I remember that when I was almost out of high school I made the decision that I was no longer going to be a Jehovah's Witness. I had experienced some hurtful situations and had really lost my desire, so I left. After graduation I got a job at MacDonald's and worked my way up to assistant manager. I had begun to sniff heroin again and many nights I would hook up with my best friend after work and get high.

At the age of nineteen, I met the man I would marry while I was going to buy drugs. That same night we hung out, and we were together ever since. Not long after, we eloped.

I continued to get high. My habit increased, and I not only was smoking and drinking, which were so normal to me, but was addicted to heroin and had begun to freebase. That's when you take cocaine and cook it up and smoke it. Eventually money became an issue, and it became harder to maintain my habit. I thought if I did the drugs intravenously, I would not need as much. So that's what I did. In time, I became multiaddictive, and it was a daily task just trying to figure out how I was going to get drugs for that day. I would lie, cheat and steal.

It got so bad that my mom would sleep with her bag under her arm because I would steal her money. Even then, I would find a way to get to it. My son was growing up, and I was becoming more and more concerned about how in the world this was ever going to stop. This addiction, how would it end? I remember the first time I began stealing from my brother, writing checks and cashing them around the corner where my family shopped and was well known. I remember losing my job because of stealing money from the register. Even though I was fired, the vice president encouraged me to go to a program and gave me money to buy drugs for the whole week so that I wouldn't be running the streets. I went to the program but never regained my job. I didn't stop doing drugs. Things continued the same until my brother called me into the room one day and asked me why I was stealing money from him. That was the first time I remember feeling really hurt. My brother was very dear to me; he worked very hard to put himself through college, and I was taking from him. I just broke down.

I told him that I wanted to go to Puerto Rico with my dad and kick. So we called my dad and a week later I was out there (Mom was still here in New York at the time). The first week was the hardest. I remember waking up throwing up, feeling sick, and having a drink to mellow the sickness. Three weeks later it was over. I had gotten over the heroin and crack addiction. Going back home was a little scary because I did not know what would happen when I got back to the place where things all started. I know many times I had cried out to God that I wanted to live a normal life, and I was getting started.

I began a new job, and my husband and I decided to get back together. (We had been separated for a little over a year.) All I knew is that I wanted a different life and it appeared that he wanted the same thing. I had already been working at the cable company for almost a year. Things were going well. My husband had begun to go to a church, which I certainly had no intentions of going to, so he challenged me to go somewhere. I remember trying to go back to the Kingdom Hall; I sat in the back and just knew this was not the place God wanted me to be. Eventually my husband began going to another church in Harlem, and I know that I felt like it was a cult. I had never heard of a church having meetings in their homes, blacks and whites together. Even with all the persecution from me, my husband decided to get baptized in the Harlem ministry of the New York City Church of Christ.

I remember after a couple of months I decided to go and visit, and I enjoyed the preaching but didn't like the singing, or should I say the amount of singing. I remember not trusting women at all because of all the things that went on in my marriage, so a lot of women would ask me to study and before they could finish, I would say no. Then one day Shawn Patterson asked if I would study, and I remember thinking I would study the Bible to prove my husband wrong. You see, I was still grounded in some of my Jehovah's Witness beliefs. By God's grace, I began studying the Bible. I remember I had to unlearn everything I knew to relearn what God's way is. It took me nine months of studying, and I thank God for the patience of all the sisters who were in my studies. I remember that because of my drug background they suggested that I go to a group called Chemical Dependency, but I said no. They, in their wisdom, did not make it an issue, but God would bring it up again in the near future.

The morning of my baptism I came home to find out that my dad had died. In my anguish, I could not understand why God would take someone so special from me. Once I had left home and got married, my dad's and my relationship had become what I'd always wanted it to be. I finally had the relationship I was always envious of between him and my older sister, and now this! I'd made the right decision, hadn't I? I was so confused. But my husband would tell me of the grace God had by bringing my dad to New York for us to spend time with him and that he did not die in Puerto Rico with my mom alone. I then understood how much God loved me.

Discipleship was awesome. I was excited, fired up, but mostly full of gratitude, and I was about to grow even in that. When I was about three months old in the faith, Robin Barnes came and asked me if I would be interested in learning how to lead Chemical Recovery (whew, thank goodness for the name change from Chemical Dependency; I couldn't stand it), and I said yes, of course. My hubby had been asked to learn how to lead the men, so that was going to be great. When I said yes, Robin said, "You know you're going to have to write a journal." No problem. Well, the problem was that although I had stopped doing drugs, I was still drinking. My thinking was: after all, Jesus drank wine, so what's the problem? That's what I kept saying to my husband, who had begun to monitor my drinking.

On the weekend, I would buy a quart of Mr. Boston's eggnog and my husband would watch how much I had drunk from day to day. So I decided that I would buy a couple of half pints, and when I would pour some into the quart container or I would just drink the half pint, then he would think I was not drinking as much. So when I wrote and read my journal, there were many drugs I had done that I said were my drugs of choice, but I never wrote about the alcohol. I always knew I was an addict, but I never thought I was an alcoholic until I started to hear journals that had to do with drinking. I saw myself in those journals and stopped drinking. I hadn't told anyone yet, but God always reveals what is hidden.

God did reveal my heart about drinking in front of a certain person and all the leaders of the chemical recovery ministry. I will never forget that day, because it was the day that God gave me a conviction about drinking. Not that I shouldn't, but that I couldn't, and from that moment on I knew that not only was I an addict but an alcoholic as well.

God has done amazing things with my life. In 1996 God brought my husband and me into the full-time ministry. We've served in the church in New York City and Los Angeles and are now back home in New York serving as regional leaders for the incredible people of the Bronx. It has been sixteen years, and Chemical Recovery is a part of my walk now as it was then. We have been all over the country training others how to lead this incredible ministry, which in reality keeps me grounded, green, and never forgetting where I come from, no matter what God is doing in my life. To God be the glory!

_____ **DREAM DARE** _____

Dare to be a woman of faith.

For Reflection: pray…ponder…promise…practice.

It's impossible to please God apart from faith. And why? Because anyone who wants to approach God must believe both that he exists and that he cares enough to respond to those who seek him. (Hebrews 11:6 MSG)

Chapter Twelve

Dare to Rise Up
for Such a Time as This

Courage is what it takes to stand up and speak; courage is also what it takes to sit down and listen. —Winston Churchill

Life isn't a matter of Milestones, but of moments. —Rose Kennedy

"And who knows whether you have not come to the kingdom for such a time as this?" (Esther 4:14b ESV)

Esther was a breathtakingly beautiful women and her beauty was used to save her own life and the lives of the Jewish people.

Her story began in 483 BC, 103 years after Nebuchadnezzar had taken the Jews into captivity. The Persians, led by Cyrus, conquered Babylon and not long after gave the Jews the freedom to return to Jerusalem or to stay in what was now part of the Persian Empire. Nearly 50,000 Jews, many of whom were devout, were in the first group to return to Jerusalem.[1]

Most likely, Jews who chose to stay in Persia after being free did so because they had established themselves and feared the dangerous journey back to their homeland. Some became comfortable in the pagan land and so assimilated into the culture that they lost their cultural and religious identity.[2]

There are so many lessons we can learn from the main characters in the book of Esther and especially from the silent main character, God. I will highlight a few of my favorites, and I encourage you if you have not spent time with Esther to set aside some time to do so.

Radiant Esther was an orphan Jew from the tribe of Benjamin. She was brought up by her much older cousin Mordecai, who was like a father to her. They were two of the Jews who remained in Persia. That fact alone tells us a lot about how she was raised.

Esther was a stranger in a strange land. Her parents died when she was a child, but she was fortunate to have kindhearted Mordecai raise her. At the time of this story, she was probably young, because women back them were usually married by their mid-teens. She stepped center stage into the world of Persia with its proud, impulsive, harsh, and drunkard king without having the advice, support, and preparation of a mom.

The book of Esther opens with a six-month-long party that King Xerxes threw to put on an extravagant display of his wealth before the military leaders, princes, and nobles of his provinces. At the end of the six months, he threw a seven-day drinking party and called in Queen Vashti in order to display her beauty to the people. She was to appear before the guests in the nude, wearing only her royal crown, according to the ancient historian Josephus.[3] Vashti refused to come, so she was banished from the king's presence for life, and a new queen was sought. An extensive search was made for beautiful young virgins who would enter the king's harem and possibly become the next queen. The search took place all over the 127 provinces over which Xerxes reigned—an even bigger area than the USA.[4] As a mother, I can't even imagine having my daughter taken for that purpose and never seeing her again. For a young woman, being snatched from home and taken to an unknown place, never to see your family again, must have been terrifying.

Subsequently, Esther was chosen to be queen, which meant keeping her heritage silent (under Mordecai's instruction), eating the king's nonkosher food, possibly pagan worship, and having slept with a man before she was married to him. Let's remember, all heroes are far from perfect. They were human and at times a hot mess, just like you and me. Their weaknesses, bad choices, and sins are exposed on the pages of the Bible so we can first, learn about God's mercy and second, be warned and encouraged by their examples. We are not to put anyone one a pedestal and we surely are in no place to judge. The only perfect person is our perfect Lord.

Fortunately, Esther went through the normal twelve months of beauty treatments before meeting the king. Whew! Thank you, God. He set aside a time for her to prepare herself. While the servants would be working on her outer beauty (excuse me; I thought the Bible said she was already aesthetically appealing?), God would be working on the inner beauty, the *"beauty of a quiet and gentle spirit,* **which is of great worth in God's sight**" (1 Peter 3:4, *emphasis added*). Isn't that just like us today? We are already beautiful in God's sight and we spend tons of time, money, effort, and anxiety to make ourselves more beautiful than what God created.

As the story continues, Haman was honored by the king and given a high position in the kingdom. He was annoyed with Mordecai because Mordecai refused to kneel down to him. Haman's anger led him to plot the execution of all the Jews in the kingdom. Dispatches were sent by couriers to all the king's provinces with the order to destroy—to kill young and old, women and children on a single day, the thirteenth day of the twelfth month.

In order to prevent the execution of all the Jews, Mordecai called on Esther to intercede with the king. The only problem here was that the king did not know that Esther was a Jew, and Esther had no idea how he would respond to this news. She sent to Mordecai saying that she was reluctant to approach the king because she knew that any man or woman who approached him in the inner court without being summoned by him was in jeopardy of being put to death. Esther had not been summoned for thirty days. Then Mordecai sent back to her an answer, this compelling truth:

> *"Do not think to yourself that in the king's palace you will escape any more than all the other Jews. For if you keep silent at this time, relief and deliverance will rise for the Jews from another place, but you and your father's house will perish. And who knows whether you have not come to the kingdom for such a time as this?"* (Esther 4:13–14)

I love it. Mordecai was not having it. He was faithful and sent what Esther needed; a great spark of insight. In my version, that verse goes something like this: "Just because you live in that palace, don't think you are all that and you alone will be saved. For if you don't speak up, don't worry; God will raise up someone else, even from another place, but you and your family are surely going down. And girl, what if the only reason you are there is for such a time as this—you will have missed your destiny!" (Shawn's Version).

I am so impressed with Esther's caution and courage in agreeing to appeal to the king. Before she approached the king, she asked Mordecai to organize a time of fasting for three days for all the Jews who were in Susa. Fasting is a godly practice in which we refrain from food to bring us closer to God. She requested that they all fast, and after the fast, she would approach the king. She was well aware that she needed God's favor if she was to succeed. That a girl, Esther! Although she had been on her own, inundated by the world, she had not forgotten who her God was and what he could do.

> *Then Esther sent this reply to Mordecai: "Go, gather together all the Jews who are in Susa, and fast for me. Do not eat or drink for three days, night or day. I and my attendants will fast as you do. When this is done, I will go to the king, even though it is against the law. And if I perish, I perish."*
> (Esther 4:15–16)

Astonishing! With that one challenge from Mordecai, Esther mustered up indomitable faith and resolved that she would face her fears, take a stand for her people, and be willing to lose her life if necessary. "If I perish, I perish" were not just words for her; given the king's character, it was a real possibility. The preparation time really helped. Esther approached the king and invited him and Haman to a banquet. She was prudent in her effort to get the timing right before she notified the king about Haman's plot to kill the Jews. The Bible says that if we lack wisdom we should ask God, who gives generously to all without finding fault (James 1:5). Esther displayed God's wisdom, foresight, trust, and patience as she waited on his timing. How often do we neglect to pray, fast, and make an effort to get the timing right before we jump into things? For the most part, when I just jump into things (even good things intended to help others) without much prayer and thought, God makes it clear that I am making a mistake, not an impact.

At last, Esther revealed to the king that she was a Jew and that Haman had plotted to kill them all. Haman was hanged on his own gallows and the Jews were delivered!

Because of Esther's and Mordecai's faithfulness and willingness to put their lives on the line, risking it all, God delivered them and all the Jews and rewarded them in unimaginable ways.

Esther's story gives us great hope that God will never forsake us. In the words of Lamentations 3:22, *"Because of the Lord's great love, we are not consumed."*

In conclusion, God is silent in the book of Esther, but you can see him working everywhere. He was working before, during and after Esther's lifetime. Her story inspires me to be willing to rise up with courage and faith for my *"such a time as this"* opportunities.

Two of our best friends in the world are Luz and Angel Martinez. The Bible says that *"a friend loves at all times"* (Proverbs 17:17), and they have truly loved us that way. Luz is one of my sheroes and reminds me of a modern-day Esther. God took an ordinary girl from the mountains in the

Dominican Republic and through the years has raised her up for such a time as this. As a result of God exalting her, her husband, and her church, a myriad of men women have heard the gospel and been saved on the island.

Luz's Story

I was born in the mountains in the north of the Dominican Republic. I was the youngest of eight children. My parents were very poor; they married and started a family in a house with a dirt floor. We had no electricity, no running water, a latrine, two hammock-like beds, and a nearby river that served as a shower where we bathed.

When I turned four, my parents moved to New York City with a dream to provide a better life for us, and my grandma kept all eight children with her. We loved the mountains, the rivers, the wooden house, the smell of the rain, all the different animals on her farm (especially chickens because whoever found the eggs owned them), the sugar cane, the mangos, and the coconuts fields. I spent the next six years of my life in the mountains climbing trees until I started school.

I believe God used my grandmother and those years with her to plant a great faith and a persevering spirit in us. One day, my sister Clary introduced God to me through prayer. She told me that when we pray, God would hear us, and I believed her. So I loved to pray and still do. I am confident God is there for me, hears me, and will always come through for me.

In 1984, when I was fifteen years old, my parents moved me to New York to live with them, and in the autumn of 1988, disciples in the Hunter College campus ministry of the New York City Church of Christ (NYCCOC) met me. After meeting them, I started studying the Bible. A month later, I was baptized and my life was forever changed.

Since that time, there are many ways in which I have seen God use me (the ordinary), to do the extraordinary.

In 1989, this ordinary girl found herself at Fashion Institute of Technology leading a group Bible discussion alongside a very talented, artistic, and sophisticated brother. Being a country girl, I knew nothing about fashion and thought I had no artistic abilities, but God was showing me that it was not about my talent or artistic ability but about knowing him. That experience built a passion for the ministry of teaching and preaching God's word and helped to prepare me for God's plans for my future.

In 1991, the NYCCOC sent me on the mission team to Puerto Rico. I remember at the first service that Jaime D'Anda, the evangelist, asked us to memorize Philippians 4:13: *"I can do all things through Christ who strengthens me"* (NKJV). This has been my theme scripture from that time. I served as a campus leader at the University of Puerto Rico, and through God's strength, many students became Christians.

To my excitement, in 1993 the NYCCOC sent yet another mission team to my home, the Dominican Republic. It was an honor to be a part of that team, and on that mission I would work alongside, fall in love with, and marry the love of my life, Angel Martinez. I am grateful for Sam and Cynthia Powell, who took me under their wings and trained me to become a great wife to Angel and women's ministry leader of the DR church. It was Cynthia who introduced me to Shawn Patterson eighteen years ago. I loved Shawn from day one, and to this day, I still value and treasure our friendship and partnership in the gospel.

The Dominican Republic is a third-world country where about forty percent of the population currently lives below the poverty level and the unemployment rate is about seventeen percent. The average national salary back then was about $150 to $300 US per month. Rents were and still are about $300 to $450 for a two-bedroom, one-bathroom apartment. Gas was about $5.50 per gallon, the electricity was scarce and expensive, and the cost of living was very high. In addition to all the difficulties, in 2003 inflation in our nation rose to over 500 percent. We thank God for the financial support the NY church provided for about nine years until the DR church could become financially self-supported.

God did miracles with the DR church that first year. We started with eighteen disciples and grew to about 100 disciples that year and 200 the second year. By the year 2000, we were almost 1000 disciples worshiping in Sunday service!

Along with the great miracles also came the great challenges. Over the past eighteen years, the DR church has faced many of them. Below are a few.

- Hurricanes and tropical storms destroyed the agriculture of the nation and brought about the destruction of homes and property, as well as the deaths of many of the disciples' family members.
- Demonstrations and protests occur frequently and at times turn violent with police responding with deadly force. Many disciples have found their lives in danger due to these events.
- Pickpocketing and muggings at gunpoint are a growing problem. Angel has experienced this firsthand, as he was mugged at gunpoint in

front of our house while he waited for a ride. We have also had our car and home broken into.

- Frequent power outages and blackouts increase crime and so make night travel very dangerous, with people having to be constantly alert and vigilant. A great number of disciples have been assaulted in public cars, and at least five sisters have been raped and others molested during blackouts. One sister was shot on her way home at night after leaving midweek service.

- Deaths have been attributed to lack of prompt medical care because of a lack of insurance or financial means. Consequently, we have seen many die of different types of cancer that may have been curable if detected earlier. Many die in childbirth, deliver stillborn babies, or lose babies to sudden infant death.

Through it all, God has worked through his people in mighty ways. He has used us and continues to use us to spread his gospel all over our island and beyond. In January 2004, we planted the Santiago Church in the north of the island and also sent the western zone region of about 130 disciples to the east of Santo Domingo. In addition, my husband and I along with eighteen disciples planted La Romana Church, at the far east of the island. As I write now, we are forming the mission team to San Juan, in the southwest part of the island about five hours from Santo Domingo.

Along with our challenges as a church, over the past twenty-four years I have faced many personal and health challenges, yet God has used me to train other women for the ministry, appoint women's ministry leaders, and influence the women leaders in the Caribbean.

Also, God has used this unschooled ordinary woman (who is presently pursuing a degree in psychology) to start a program called English and More, which focuses on teaching adults and teens the English language and helps them pursue their personal dreams. As part of the "more" of the program, God has used me and six other disciples to get teens baptized, restore spouses, train singles in the work of the ministry, train more women's leaders and missionaries, and help people get better jobs. God also used me to create Fun Ways, a summer camp of which I am the founder and director. The camp focuses on helping parents target the spiritual and psychological needs of their children in order to provide better counseling and spiritual guidance throughout the rest of the year.

_____ DREAM DARE _____

Dare to be brave, strong and fearless when pursuing your dream. The Lord your God will always be by your side!

For Reflection: pray…ponder…promise…practice.

> *"Be brave and strong! Don't be afraid of the nations on the other side of the Jordan. The LORD your God will always be at your side, and he will never abandon you."* (Deuteronomy 31:6 CEV)

Chapter Thirteen

Dare to Use Your Gifts
to Build Up the Body

We make a living by what we get. We make a life by what we give.
—Winston Churchill

*For by the grace given me I say to every one of you: Do not think of
yourself more highly than you ought, but rather think of yourself with
sober judgment, in accordance with the faith God has distributed to each
of you. For just as each of us has one body with many members, and these
members do not all have the same function, so in Christ we, though many,
form one body, and each member belongs to all the others. We have different
gifts, according to the grace given to each of us. If your gift is prophesying,
then prophesy in accordance with your faith; if it is serving, then serve; if
it is teaching, then teach; if it is to encourage, then give encouragement; if
it is giving, then give generously; if it is to lead, do it diligently; if it is to
show mercy, do it cheerfully.* (Romans 12:3–8)

God has graciously given the members of his body his spiritual gifts
(charisma) and distributed them throughout the church. Yes, dear friend,
everyone has at least one gift, and some are multigifted. Our Father in his
supreme wisdom and generosity works powerfully through his church, en-
dowing it with a plethora of gifts so the church can accomplish its work (John
17:4). That's mind-blowing to me. In 1 Peter 4:10 God says he expects each
one of us to use our gifts not just for our benefit but to serve others, and he
calls us to be faithful stewards of God's Grace. Do you know what your gift
is? Are you using it to accomplish the work of the church?

Incidentally, the Bible teaches that God sends his gifts and blessings on Christians and non-Christians alike: *"He causes his sun to rise on the evil and the good, and sends rain on the righteous and the unrighteous"* (Matthew 5:45). There are many gifts cited in the Bible, and for a helpful resource with more information, please see *The Spirit* by Douglas Jacoby.[1]

I have been so enlightened, encouraged, and challenged from the first day I met Paul on the pages of the New Testament. He himself was multigifted and had a burning passion for his relationship with Jesus and God's dream for his life. That compelled him to travel throughout the Roman Empire telling others about Christ.

> *We set sail from Troas and took a straight course to Samothrace, the following day to Neapolis, and from there to Philippi, which is a leading city of the district of Macedonia and a Roman colony. We remained in this city for some days. On the sabbath day we went outside the gate by the river, where we supposed there was a place of prayer; and we sat down and spoke to the women who had gathered there. A certain woman named Lydia, a worshiper of God, was listening to us; she was from the city of Thyatira and a dealer in purple cloth. The Lord opened her heart to listen eagerly to what was said by Paul. When she and her household were baptized, she urged us, saying, "If you have judged me to be faithful to the Lord, come and stay at my home." And she prevailed upon us.* (Acts 16:11–15 NRSV)

While Paul was in Troas, on the coast of Asia Minor, he *"had a vision of a man of Macedonia standing and begging him, 'Come over to Macedonia and help us'"* (Acts 16:9). Paul humbly trusted and followed the Holy Spirit who was leading him to Macedonia. He chose to go to Philippi with a plan to reach the rest of Macedonia because Philippi was the key city in the region. When he and his traveling companions arrived in Philippi, there was inscribed on the arches outside the city a prohibition against bringing an unrecognized religion into the city.[2] Despite its size, Philippi hadn't had enough Jews to provide the requisite quorum of ten reliable males to form a synagogue, so Paul headed to the river where he knew Jews would gather when they were unable to go to a synagogue.[3] There they found a group of faithful women meeting to worship. Lydia was at the river. She was *"a worshiper of God,"* and listened to Paul's teachings. In fact, we are told that *"the Lord opened her heart to listen eagerly to what was said by Paul."* She and her household were baptized, and she urged Paul and his fellow travelers to stay in her house. Lydia was the first convert to Christianity in Europe. Acts 16:40 implies that by the end of Paul's stay in Philippi, the first church planted in Europe, a new church was meeting in Lydia's home.

Lydia seemed to have it all. She was a rich, illustrious career woman who owned her house, had servants, and was hospitable. But Lydia was missing something. She was empty, not satisfied, and needed to be made whole, and God saw and met her deepest need. It must have been out of sheer gratitude that she immediately started using her gifts to serve God and his people.

Lydia's baptism was the beginning of a new life of using her many spiritual gifts. Evidently, she had the gift of leadership. She not only was baptized but also influenced those in her household to be baptized, which would have included servants. In addition, she had the gift of hospitality, which she immediately used to provide lodging for the missionaries and a place for this new church to meet.

Professionally, Lydia was a prosperous businesswoman. She was a *"dealer in purple cloth"* from Thyatira. Thyatira was the capitol of the industry and renowned for its purple dyes. One had to have plenty of capital to deal in purple dye and the making of purple garments for sale. Purple dye was a symbol of power and honor in the ancient world, and it was the most expensive and sought-after dye in the Roman world.

Being successful is not wrong or sinful. If you are blessed with ability, creativity, and a strong work ethic, and God has blessed that with wealth, I say, "Hallelujah!" Just remember a few things:

The Purpose: *"From everyone who has been given much, much will be demanded; and from the one who has been entrusted with much, much more will be asked."* (Luke 12:48)

The Provider: *"You may say to yourself, 'My power and the strength of my hands have produced this wealth for me.' But remember the LORD your God, for it is he who gives you the ability to produce wealth, and so confirms his covenant, which he swore to your ancestors, as it is today."* (Deuteronomy 8:17–18)

The Priority: *"Command those who are rich in this present world not to be arrogant nor to put their hope in wealth, which is so uncertain, but to put their hope in God, who richly provides us with everything for our enjoyment. Command them to do good, to be rich in good deeds, and to be generous and willing to share."* (1 Timothy 6:17–1)

I am reminded of Lydia when I think of mi amiga Jacqueline. I had the pleasure of meeting her when Mike and I were first invited to visit the great church in the Dominican Republic. She and her husband were just two of the people there whose generosity and heart is to use all of their gifts to serve the kingdom. They have made an eternal impact on my heart and in countless numbers of lives.

Jacqueline's Story

When I studied the Bible and became a Christian at the age of twenty-one, my dream was to use my career and talents to develop a profitable business that would give me a life of material abundance. I would often be late for church and at times would not even attend because I was involved in my business. My friends at church helped me to see that my heart was more committed to my love of money than it was to taking care of my relationship with God. The Scripture says in Matthew 6:24, *"No one can serve two masters. Either you will hate the one and love the other, or you will be devoted to the one and despise the other. You cannot serve both God and money."* With time, I began to understand that I should serve my master, Jesus, above everything else in this world. The scripture in 1 Peter 4:10 also helped me to understand that my gifts and possessions were given to me by God—not just for my personal benefit, but also so that I would administer them and use them to serve my neighbor.

Today at thirty-seven, I am a wife, mother, and civil engineer. My husband, who is also a disciple, is an architect. Together we have worked on several government and commercial projects.

I am very grateful to God, for through his word he has been transforming my selfish heart into one that greatly desires to serve him with all the resources he has given me. Once my heart changed, I began to see the many ways God could use me to serve his people and advance his kingdom. In the following paragraphs, I will share some of the ways that God has worked through my career, economic resources, and talent to change my part of the world: my country, the Dominican Republic.

I've sent you Huram-Abi—he's already on his way—he knows the construction business inside and out. His mother is from Dan and his father from Tyre. He knows how to work in gold, silver, bronze, iron, stone, and wood, in purple, violet, linen, and crimson textiles; he is also an expert engraver and competent to work out designs with your artists and architects, and those of my master David, your father. (2 Chronicles 2:12–14 MSG)

Building Homes

Through the years, my husband and I have had the opportunity to build homes for my three siblings and my husband's mother. We have also built and remodeled homes and apartments for disciples, charging only about thirty percent of the actual project cost.

For years, I had a desire to build my dream mansion, and in 2000 we were blessed with an opportunity to do so. As we began to think and pray, I recalled how I had seen my minister and his wife use their home to serve the Lord with fervent hearts but how they had to continually change their place of residence because of ministry needs, high rent, and landlord complaints. Since they had no home of their own, their living situations were not conducive to the work they were trying to accomplish.

With that in mind, I shared with my husband the idea that God placed on my heart to put aside the dream mansion that I desired and instead build two small, moderate homes so that we could sell one of them to our minister at an affordable price. And so we did!

It has been amazing to see how God has used and is using our twin houses for his glory. We have entertained in our homes dozens of couples, singles, campus students, and teens who have been able to study the Bible and get baptized.

God has also allowed me to personally fight through and overcome my struggle with anxiety when it comes to the things in our home getting ruined as we host events. Instead, we decided that if necessary we would annually change our furniture and anything else that would wear down, but we would never stop serving the Lord with our home due to being stressed over what could get ruined or damaged, for the Scripture says in Luke 16:9, *"I tell you, use your worldly wealth to gain friends for yourselves, so that when it is gone, you will be welcomed into eternal dwellings."*

God has truly been in control, because nothing in my house has ever been ruined by either the children or the adults that visit us. Today, I have the firm conviction that wherever I live now or in the future, I will use it with the same purpose for which the apostle Paul used his home: *"For two whole years Paul stayed there in his own rented house and welcomed all who came to see him. He proclaimed the kingdom of God and taught about the Lord Jesus Christ—with all boldness and without hindrance!"* (Acts 28:30–31).

We Built the Temple

A couple of years ago I started dreaming about constructing a church building so that our church could have a permanent place to worship. I shared this dream with my husband and it fascinated him. Since we knew that the church did not have the means for such a big project, my husband and I decided to offer our professional services free of charge. The idea was well received by the church, but we were in need of more than just our professional skills; the church needed money to see the project through. My husband and I decided to donate a fair amount of money, and many others who were encouraged by our sacrifice were inspired to do the same. It was a great sacrifice, but we still needed more funds, so I encouraged the church to do garage sales, which brought in a great amount of revenue, and soon after we were able to buy a piece of land. My husband had already designed the building, but we still needed more money to begin the construction. It was then that we, along with several other couples, decided to refinance our homes so that we could lend the money to the church to finish the construction of the building. The church is responsible for paying the mortgages, but all the couples committed to take responsibility for the loans if the church would ever fail to pay.

We were finally able to complete the construction of our majestic temple, which has brought much joy, much fruit, and great stability to the church. It has been used for services, workshops, special events like men's forums and women's days, Christmas shows, and a toy giveaway for the kids of the neighborhood during which over 300 toys were given away. We held a memorial service there for a new brother who shortly after being converted found out he had stage 4 cancer but was able to see his wife and daughter baptized before he passed. We have held all-night prayers there as well, and weddings—lots of weddings! The building at this moment is eighty-five percent paid off: we only owe $150,000 on a one-million-dollar construction.

We Built a School

As my sister (who is also a disciple) and I began our search for a good school for our children, we found ourselves changing from one school to another year after year. We were growing more and more concerned as we realized that the spiritual and moral values of our educational institutions had completely disappeared.

Even though both our families had made financial provisions so that our children could attend the best schools in our country, we decided to unite our savings to tackle the problem. We purchased a school and took time out from our own profitable businesses to invest ourselves in the development of yet another meaningful project. Both families made the decision to be physically and emotionally involved in the school on a daily basis. Our desire was to provide for our children and the children of those parents who would trust us to offer a complete education with Christian values as the foundation of character development.

I should say here that we do not financially benefit from this project, because the monthly fee is set at a rate most of the parents in our congregation can afford. I can also say that the benefits we have received are priceless. Imagine the great joy and happiness I receive from having the opportunity to spend the whole day at the school where my daughter and the children of my congregation attend. I totally enjoy the opportunity to watch over them and guide their development in the school environment.

In addition, it is of great honor for me to be a part of an educational institution where we can uphold biblical principles and create an atmosphere where parents and students understand and agree to hold to our school statutes (which include antibullying rules).

I have reached the conclusion that there are things in this life that no amount of money or property could ever give us. I have never worked so hard and for so many hours without receiving pay, yet I have never been more proud of anything. We are barely a year and a half into this project, and we have a student body of 200 children whose parents have regained hope because their children are receiving an education that reinforces the biblical principles and heart they are teaching at home.

I have the conviction that the best inheritance I could give to my daughter is my time, the security from growing up emotionally healthy, and the provision of everything she needs to rid her of any obstacle that may keep her from having a relationship with God.

Building Lives

In a developing country there are always families in need of food and medicine for their children, so God moved our hearts to contribute generously to our church's monthly budget, which consistently gives to those in need.

We also use our resources to help pay for the travel expenses of some of our guest speakers and teachers who come to the Dominican Republic to encourage the church and give workshops to our congregation.

Finally, I have become convinced that I will only have one chance to serve God and my neighbors and that time is definitely now, while I am alive. I feel at peace knowing that I have really used my career, resources, and God-given gifts at least to contribute in the slightest way to the advancement of the kingdom of God here on earth. I desire to live the rest of the days of my life thinking and behaving according to this scripture: *"I do all this for the sake of the gospel, that I may share in its blessings"* (1 Corinthians 9:23).

DREAM DARE

Dare to use your gifts well. Start now!

For Reflection: pray…ponder…promise…practice.

Each of you has been blessed with one of God's many wonderful gifts to be used in the service of others. So use your gift well. (1 Peter 4:10 CEV)

Chapter Fourteen

Dare to Be Phenomenal in Your Youth

The young do not know enough to be prudent, and therefore they attempt the impossible—and achieve it, generation after generation.
—Pearl S. Buck

Remember your Creator
  in the days of your youth. (Ecclesiastes 12:1a)

Don't let anyone look down on you because you are young, but set an example for the believers in speech, in conduct, in love, in faith and in purity. (1 Timothy 4:12)

Whether you are thirteen or thirty, the scripture in 1 Timothy above is for you and me. Hold on, let's not just read up to *"Don't let anyone look down on you because you are young,"* seeing as there are pearls of wisdom that follow. Often these five areas—speech, conduct, love, faith, and purity—are the key areas in which not only young people, but honestly, not-so-young people struggle.

I am so excited for the young people reading this chapter. The sky is the limit for how God can use you if your start now. The best way to begin pursuing your dreams, no matter what they are, is to strive to set a Christlike example in those five areas.

My friend Jordan was eighteen when I first met her in the fellowship at church. She was a new member in the GACC campus ministry and was full of zest and zeal. Several things stood out about Jordan, such as her pure love for God, her brilliance, and her inner and outer beauty. On top of that, I look up to her because she has been a young woman who has striven to set an example in the five areas above, and God has already been revealing and blessing the dreams she has been pursuing for his Glory.

Jordan's Story

When I look back on my childhood, the happy memories that come to mind seem endless. One of these memories is the precious little pearl of wisdom that my mom, a kindergarten teacher for much of my upbringing, always shared with my younger brother and me when we were kids: "Always do the maximum, never the minimum!" I could hear my mom's sweet voice in my head whenever there was an extra-credit assignment, an opportunity to complete homework a week before it was due, or even a chance to volunteer to stay behind and help a teacher tidy up after all of the other kids had left. God used both her and my father powerfully to plant countless seeds that have helped to shape my deep convictions on serving and glorifying God with excellence.

What I respect so much about my parents is that they showed me far more about diligence and consistency than they ever told me. My father, an attorney, would read the book of Proverbs with us before our bedtime to teach us the value of wisdom and hard work, then he would give us a living example of both as he went on to mull over contracts for hours until he fell asleep himself. Because of my parents' examples, I was passionately determined to put in the work so that I could become the best student I could possibly be, not because I was afraid of how my parents would react to a less-than-stellar report card, but because I had chosen to adopt excellence as my own standard. I was inspired, never coerced, to have high expectations for myself, and I am forever grateful to my parents for that.

After receiving acceptance letters from some incredible universities, I decided (correction: God decided!) that I would attend Spelman College in Atlanta, Georgia. Having never lived outside of a twenty-five-mile radius of my hometown of Washington, DC, I found college to be an even bigger adjustment than I thought it would be. At the age of eighteen, I found myself disillusioned and searching for answers in a way that I never had before. Somehow, my goals of graduating at the top of my class, going on to a top law school, landing a nice job, and having a nice family—all of which, of course, would be incomplete without a relationship with God in the mix—seemed more like a sensible ten-year plan that would give me a cushy life than a real dream that would impact the lives of others. While I did not have all of the answers, I did know that my frustration stemmed from my relationship with God being a piece of the puzzle when it was intended to be the entire picture. My soul was crying out for more of Jesus, and after wrestling with the Scriptures and striving to implement them in every area of my life, I discovered the liberating truth of what it means to make him Lord of my life. I was beyond ready to submit to his perfect plan for me as outlined in his word and embrace whatever direction it would take my life. I was baptized at eighteen in February 2008, and I have been living life to the full ever since!

Since that time, I have absolutely loved sharing with other young women what had been shared with me, and serving in the campus—and, currently, the teen—ministries. As law school loomed over my not-so-distant future, I began to view it as a burden that would take away from my ministry of reconciliation, rather than a blessing that would give me the story I needed to share with others the dream I did not yet know I had. I thought, "A great daughter to you, a great future wife to my amazing fiancé, a great mother to our future children, a great law student, a great support to my family, a great sister to the women whose lives I'm investing in...almost all of which would be happening at the same time?! God, are there really enough hours in the day?" During moments of clarity, I gave up that battle and chose to fix my eyes on Jesus and trust him to take care of the rest.

It was then that I began to get a glimpse of my dream: to inspire women at all stages and from all walks of life to pursue excellence in every area of their lives, be they housewives, single mothers, women's ministry leaders, or corporate executives! To encourage them that if they love our God—for whom nothing is impossible—with all of their hearts, souls, minds, and strength, then that love will overflow into every area of their lives, they will be inspired to work hard and give their very best in every role they play, and they will *"serve before kings, [and] will not serve before obscure men"* (Proverbs 22:29), who in turn will know that we serve an awesome God! This is what stirs my soul. This is my dream, and I knew that I could not share it if I chose not to live it. As if to confirm all of this, our father allowed me to graduate from Spelman as the valedictorian of my class! As a result, I experienced the privilege of meeting the incredible First Lady of the USA, Mrs. Michelle Obama; and Ms. Phylicia Rashad, the marvelous actor who played Clair Huxtable in the Cosby Show, all in the same afternoon. It was an honor to meet the First Lady, and meeting Phylicia Rashad was so special to me because, along with my mom, Clair had always been my role model growing up. Her role as a captivating, smart-as-a-whip wife, mother, and high-powered attorney represented the type of woman I always wanted to be.

Today, I am a twenty-three-year-old, beyond happily married second-year law student still making an impact on teenagers and immersed in a world of readings that seem to have no end and sleep that seems to have no beginning, but I know that I am pursuing a dream that has no limits! I have already been offered positions at prestigious law firms in Georgia, but I do not have it all together and am convinced that I never will (especially once we become parents!). I stand in awe of God during those frequent reminders that he is the only explanation for why I am hard pressed on every side, but not crushed (2 Corinthians 4:8). The desire of my heart is to make my father smile in every role that he allows me to fulfill and to inspire other women to strive to do everything well, just like Jesus did (Mark 7:37).

_____ **DREAM DARE** _____

Dare to dream for God while you are still young.

For Reflection: pray...ponder...promise...practice.

> *Remember your Creator*
> *in the days of your youth,*
> *before the days of trouble come*
> *and the years approach when you will say,*
> *"I find no pleasure in them."* (Ecclesiastes 12:1)

Chapter Fifteen

Dare to Remember the Poor

There is no exercise better for the heart than reaching down and lifting people up. —John Holmes

We are prone to judge success by the index of our salaries or by the size of our automobiles rather than by the quality of our service and relationship to mankind. —Dr. Martin Luther King Jr.

John replied, "If you have two shirts, give one to the poor. If you have food, share it with those who are hungry." (Luke 3:11 NLT)

In Joppa there was a disciple named Tabitha (in Greek her name is Dorcas); she was always doing good and helping the poor. About that time she became sick and died, and her body was washed and placed in an upstairs room. Lydda was near Joppa; so when the disciples heard that Peter was in Lydda, they sent two men to him and urged him, "Please come at once!"

Peter went with them, and when he arrived he was taken upstairs to the room. All the widows stood around him, crying and showing him the robes and other clothing that Dorcas had made while she was still with them.

Peter sent them all out of the room; then he got down on his knees and prayed. Turning toward the dead woman, he said, "Tabitha, get up." She opened her eyes, and seeing Peter she sat up. He took her by the hand and helped her to her feet. Then he called for the believers, especially the widows, and presented her to them alive. This became known all over Joppa, and many people believed in the Lord. (Acts 9:36–42)

Talk about leaving a legacy! The first time we meet Dorcas, she is dead and we are learning from her life. Her name tells us she lived in two worlds—the Greek world and the Jewish world. Dorcas was her Greek name, and Greek is the language she would have spoken on the street, in the marketplace, and while doing business. Tabitha, which is Aramaic, was her Jewish name, and Aramaic would have been spoken at home and in more intimate relationships.[1] It's not surprising that Dorcas would stand out to Luke in particular, because Luke mentions women more than any other gospel writer, mentioning their presence in the life of Jesus and the contributions they made to his ministry.[2] Luke calls Dorcas a disciple, and this is the only time the New Testament uses the term "disciple" to describe a woman. Obviously, she reminded people of Jesus' compassion and his heart to serve the poor.

Living by the sea, Dorcas saw numerous fathers and husbands venture into the perilous waters and never return. Left behind were bereaved and often destitute widows who were forced to beg or become prostitutes to survive and take care of their children.[3] Seeing this must have broken Dorcas's heart, and as she became impassioned to reach out to them, God's dream for her was born. One of the ways she served them was by making robes and other clothes for the widows and maybe the poor, which was not a quick or easy undertaking. In that day and time there were no sewing machines, no Jo-Ann Fabric and Craft Stores, no Michaels' and no Hobby Lobby. Her work would have entailed spinning fiber into thread to weave on her loom into cloth before sewing clothing for others. She may have also had to support herself, since the Bible does not mention a husband. When she died, it was a great loss, and the disciples were so moved they sent two men to Lydda to urge Peter to come quickly to Joppa. Since we read in Galatians 2:10 that it was very important to the apostles that people remember the poor, I can imagine Peter being eager to meet this woman who had the reputation of *"always doing good and helping the poor."* It is not unusual for people to do good deeds. I think most people can say they do good deeds here and there, and as disciples we are expected to abound in them (2 Corinthians 9:8), but to be a disciple who is always doing good deeds is extraordinary.

When Peter arrived, he went to Dorcas's room and it was full of widows mourning and showing the clothing she had made for them. Peter cleared the room, got on his knees and prayed, and gave her a second chance at life just as she had given so many of those women and children. And when she was brought back to life, it became known all over Joppa and many people believed. She made a colossal impact on her community in life and in returning from death.

While reading this, I had an epiphany. So many times, we know there are needs in our church, in our homes, and in our communities, but we wait for someone to tell us what to do or to ask us to do it. I just love Dorcas's pure and simple heart: she saw a need in her community, opened her heart, and went above and beyond to meet it. She needed no fanfare, no praise, and no accolades. She used her own gifts and talents to nurture a group of women who desperately needed it. It was a way of life for her and God's dream for her.

I am overjoyed for you to meet two women who are remarkable friends of mine. Liana Sisco is one of my newer friends. You know the saying, "Make new friends but keep the old; one is silver and the other gold?" I am so fond of my silver friends! Our relationship is one of those that clicked from our first meeting. She makes me smile, laugh and cry, and she convicts the tar out of me. Her daughter Shelly, who is deaf and has cerebral palsy, is a very special member of our church family. She reminds us all of God's unconditional love, and her constant smile is contagious, causing us all to be joyful always. My friend Liana is a modern-day Dorcas and is currently living her dream serving the elderly and the poor at a nonprofit senior living facility in Atlanta.

Liana's story

I met my husband, Burke, twenty-five years ago in Huntsville, Alabama at the Central Church of Christ. I was a single mom with a chronically ill baby who is deaf and has cerebral palsy. I've always been so amazed at how Burke was given the opportunity to choose his child and he chose one who (in a worldly sense) was far less than perfect. Over the years, this has been a constant reminder to me of how God chose me and has always seen me as precious even though I am far less than perfect. As a matter of fact, before my husband and I were dating, I was alone in the car when the Billy Joel song "She's Got a Way" began playing. I told God, "It would be great if someday someone felt that way about me." A couple of years later when we were planning our wedding, Burke asked if he could sing that very song to me during our ceremony. All I could do was cry. I had never told anyone about the secret wish I had shared with God!

In 1999, we were introduced to an amazing ministry for special-needs kids and their families. We attended a seminar at the San Francisco Church of Christ where we witnessed the incredible power in the lives of people who normally feel so powerless. I came back to Atlanta determined that we would have a ministry like that. I bought Rubbermaid tubs and some special toys for the disabled kids in our ministry. Every Sunday I visited each class and taught the teachers and typical kids how to interact with the special-needs kids in a meaningful way. I plugged away, and in a few months we had a thriving ministry with a class of our own and a parent support network. The disciples in the Atlanta church were thrilled to volunteer and led these kids to some amazing victories!

In 2001, we moved to Hampton, Georgia. I eventually took a job at a nursing home where I worked for seven years. For the first two weeks of my employment, I cried hysterically every day on my way home from work. My heart was breaking. People are suffering in ways I had never even considered. I was determined to be a light in that dark place. Some of the residents were in a vegetative state, so when I talked to them I prayed that they would be comforted. I hoped they would think an angel was talking to them and realize that God hadn't forgotten them.

During our time in Hampton, we became board members for People First of Henry County, a group devoted to encouraging the disabled and their families. One of the events they sponsored every year was a special-needs pageant. There was a "Mr. and Miss Special Henry County" and they were in parades and signed autographs. It was incredible! Our daughter was Miss Special Henry County, 2008. The following year, our family was honored as recipients of the Volunteer of the Year Award.

When we lived in the suburbs, we would drive to the city with lunches to hand out to the homeless. We quickly came to the conviction that our actions created dysfunctional relationships with the ones we wanted to serve. Our intentions were good, to be sure, but a handout is not what they need. What they really need is a relationship. We were determined to move into the city where we could be neighbors of people in need—part of the community.

We now live in a very densely populated and diverse community in Atlanta. Our deep desire is to connect with as many people as possible, so I became "The Soup Mama." I make spectacular soup every week, which people order on my blog. I deliver the soup by bicycle to front porches and coolers. (I'm exactly like the milkman—only it's soup.) People pay a donation for my wares and I give away some soup every week. It's a good thing: fresh, organic, and locally sourced (when available) homemade soup delivered to your door weekly. I deliver the soup in one-quart mason jars (two huge servings) along with fabulous bread. I cook on Monday and deliver on Tuesday. If you're not home, no worries: just leave a small cooler and the Soup Mama will deposit the soup there. The next week, when I deliver your new soup I'll pick up last week's mason jar…just like the milkman!

I recently had a dream come true when I became the activities coordinator for a nonprofit senior living facility. The organization I work for diligently works to provide housing for poor seniors, and we work equally hard to keep them out of nursing homes. This facility is right in my neighborhood!

So I'm the Soup Mama and the adopted daughter of many seniors. God has truly been gracious to me in making a way for me to actively love what he loves.

Here are a few of the things we do that may also work well in your community:

- We volunteer in our community with: the Atlanta BeltLine, where we've done a bunch of cleanups and helped with information booths at festivals; the Old Fourth Ward Neighborhood Planning Unit doing neighborhood cleanups; and Year of Boulevard (YoBoulevard!) cleanups specifically on Boulevard. When we see an area that needs cleaning, sometimes we just go out on our own with garbage bags.
- We try not to leave our neighborhood to eat out or shop. Every Laundromat, restaurant, coffee shop, or grocery store we visit is an opportunity to build relationships. We meet with brothers and sisters out in our neighborhood rather than in our house. We want to be known, and we especially want people to feel like we know them. The last time I met a sister at The Corner Tavern for lunch, our server pulled up a chair and sat down to talk! I am so encouraged that she feels that comfortable with me.
- We've found the library to be a good place to meet homeless people, especially in the winter. We've made several friends at our neighborhood library. As a matter of fact, Shelly is famous with the librarians!

Scoutmob did an online video interview with me, Georgia State University did an article (it was so sweet and cute), Patch East Atlanta did an online video interview, there was an article in *Ponce Press,* and Fox 5 did a piece on me. When I interviewed with Lutheran Towers senior housing community, the staff kept saying, "I saw this interview..." or "I read about you in..." SO FUNNY!

Deirdre Delany Daniel, whom I have known for over twenty years, is one of my bosom buddies. I have always admired her brilliance and her determination to not let her health challenges prevent her from doing all that God had and still has in store for her as she serves the poor orphans and children in Cambodia.

Deidre's Story

I was fortunate to grow up in a family that counted its blessings, and I was taught that we always had something to give. I grew up volunteering from a very young age, whether that was going door-to-door to collect money for the March of Dimes or volunteering in the local hospital in my teens. I had a dream of doing something with my life that would make a difference in the lives of others. I became a Christian while I was in nursing school, and God put it on my heart to go into the Peace Corps. Health challenges prevented me from doing that, and life followed a different course. I thought my opportunity to serve in that way had passed. I later married and had children but still had a dream to do something "bigger." God had blessed me with a man who had similar dreams, but given that I still had my health challenges and now had a family as well, I was certain my dream would instead become a regret. The final straw came years later when the loss of my infant daughter left me feeling like I had nothing left to give. I thought my dreams were gone. That is, until I had a chance to see my life through someone else's eyes.

For years, as we had done everything just to get through life, hanging on and grasping for moments of joy in the little things, my husband was steadily gaining experience in healthcare administration in rural Alaska, which is very much a third-world setting. Because of this experience, he was invited to do some volunteer work in Cambodia, and I was able to go volunteer with him. There we met a widow with AIDS. She was living in a slum with her seven children. She had recently lost her infant daughter, yet she begged me to adopt her son and take him to America so she would not have to watch another child die. She looked at me and saw that I had plenty to give, and that spark ignited a bonfire within me. What was once a dream of something I wanted to do became something I must do. God had not forgotten my dream; he had been using the challenges in my life to make me more suited for the work he had all planned out for me to do. He was also equipping my husband and partner with the skills necessary for the task. Since I met that grieving widow more than ten years ago, God has given my family the opportunity to live and work in mainland China and to adopt two beautiful girls from there. We spent our time helping hundreds of orphans and children living in poverty to access healthcare and proper nutrition. Moreover, we have been able to share with so many others the reason we serve as we share the love of Christ with those whom the world views as unlovable. We are now on our way back to Cambodia to live and work there. I am grateful to serve a God who out of his abundance has shared all he has with me, for he has given me more than enough to share with others.

DREAM DARE

Dare to give to those who can't give back.

For Reflection: pray…ponder…promise…practice.

Then he turned to the host. "The next time you put on a dinner, don't just invite your friends and family and rich neighbors, the kind of people who will return the favor. Invite some people who never get invited out, the misfits from the wrong side of the tracks. You'll be—and experience—a blessing. They won't be able to return the favor, but the favor will be returned—oh, how it will be returned!—at the resurrection of God's people." (Luke 14:13-14 MSG)

Chapter Sixteen

Dare to Be Devoted
to One Another

It is by chance that we met, by choice that we became friends.
—Henri Nouwen

A friend loves at all times. (Proverbs 17:17a)

I consider the book of Ruth to be overflowing with the most incandescently beautiful love stories in the Bible: the love of God for man, the love between Ruth (whose name means friend) and Naomi, and the love between Boaz and Ruth. When I married Mike, I used the famous quote from Ruth 1:16 in my wedding vows: *"Where you go I will go, and where you stay I will stay. Your people will be my people and your God my God."*

In the days when the judges ruled, there was a famine in the land. So a man from Bethlehem in Judah, together with his wife and two sons, went to live for a while in the country of Moab. The man's name was Elimelek, his wife's name was Naomi, and the names of his two sons were Mahlon and Kilion. They were Ephrathites from Bethlehem, Judah. And they went to Moab and lived there.

Now Elimelek, Naomi's husband, died, and she was left with her two sons. They married Moabite women, one named Orpah and the other Ruth. After they had lived there about ten years, both Mahlon and Kilion also died, and Naomi was left without her two sons and her husband. (Ruth 1:1–5)

The Book of Ruth transpires during the time of Judges. It was a time when each man did what he saw fit, and complete chaos, idolatry, sin, and infidelity ensued. This story of love, loyalty, and fidelity shone brightly in a dark place.

At this time there was a famine in Judah. Elimelek, his wife Naomi, and their two sons were from the tribe of Ephraim but were living in Bethlehem in the middle of Judah. They left there in desperation and went to live in Moab, followers of God searching for refuge from the famine.

Moab was sin city. They practiced idol (Baal) worship and they bowed down to gods of wood and stone. Since Jews were prohibited from having any association with pagans and were forbidden to intermarry with the Moabites, it was out of the frying pan into the fire for them!

Then life threw some curve balls, as it usually does, and while in Moab, Naomi's husband died, her two sons married Moabite women, and after living there ten years, her two sons died. We can speculate as to why God took all the men in the family, but the bottom line is that most of us can hardly fathom the pain, suffering, fear, insecurity, and disappointment that derives from unexpected death, shattered dreams, loss of providers, and squelched hope, all in a foreign country.

When Naomi heard in Moab that the LORD had come to the aid of his people by providing food for them, she and her daughters-in-law prepared to return home from there. With her two daughters-in-law she left the place where she had been living and set out on the road that would take them back to the land of Judah.

Then Naomi said to her two daughters-in-law, "Go back, each of you, to your mother's home. May the LORD show you kindness, as you have shown kindness to your dead husbands and to me. May the LORD grant that each of you will find rest in the home of another husband."

Then she kissed them goodbye and they wept aloud and said to her, "We will go back with you to your people."

But Naomi said, "Return home, my daughters. Why would you come with me? Am I going to have any more sons, who could become your husbands? Return home, my daughters; I am too old to have another husband. Even if I thought there was still hope for me—even if I had a husband tonight and then gave birth to sons—would you wait until they grew up? Would you remain unmarried for them? No, my daughters. It is more bitter for me than for you, because the LORD's hand has turned against me!"

At this they wept aloud again. Then Orpah kissed her mother-in-law goodbye, but Ruth clung to her.

"Look," said Naomi, "your sister-in-law is going back to her people and her gods. Go back with her." (Ruth 1:6–15)

Naomi heard that the Lord had provided food for his people and the famine in Israel was over. Now that her husband and her sons were dead, she longed to go home. So Naomi and her daughters-in-law set off to return to the land of Bethlehem, about a seven- to ten-day walk.

I love the relationship that existed between Naomi and the brides (the same Hebrew word means bride and daughter-in-law[1]). It seems as though Orpah and Ruth each had an exceptional relationship with their husband's mother and that they were kind to each other. They remind me of my relationship with my mother-in-law, which has been so refreshing. Although she already has ten children, with three girls of her own, she has always made me feel wanted and has considered me like her own daughter. Thanks, Mom.

Understandably, when tragedy strikes, it takes a heavy toll on us. Even though Naomi was struggling with bitterness, sorrow and hardship, she still desired to look out for the brides' needs. It would have been to her benefit to have the younger women accompany her to Judah, but she pled with them to go to their mothers' homes so that each might find rest in the home of a husband. Even if Naomi were married and were to conceive that very night, Orpah and Ruth would be old women before the sons would have aged enough to marry. Orpah loved Naomi and did not want to leave, but she knew that she wanted to remarry, so she kissed Naomi goodbye, but Ruth clung to her mother-in-law. Ruth was determined to go with Naomi, and nothing Naomi said would change her mind.

But Ruth replied, "Don't urge me to leave you or to turn back from you. Where you go I will go, and where you stay I will stay. Your people will be my people and your God my God. Where you die I will die, and there I will be buried. May the LORD deal with me, be it ever so severely, if even death separates you and me." When Naomi realized that Ruth was determined to go with her, she stopped urging her. (Ruth 1:16–18)

Did you catch this, friends? What makes a woman want to follow another, stay with them, adapt to another culture, serve their God, and then vow to die together? Ruth had developed a fierce love and loyalty, and as a result she was motivated to leave everything: her home, people, culture, and even her dream to marry again sometime in her life. She lost a husband but found what she was looking for, the God of Abraham, Isaac, Jacob, and Naomi. She was, first and foremost, eager to cling to the God she had fallen in love with.

To be sure, you can't assign these kinds of relationships, mandate them, or designate them. You have to *build* them. There are no shortcuts. It takes time and two people who are willing to make the investment. Perhaps Ruth had been watching her new family and at some point Naomi's God became her God. She saw God as Naomi's God, and she yearned for that relationship, with all its good, bad and ugly moments. That takes transparency and vulnerability. In all of this, Ruth also found **a** woman whom she admired, respected and trusted, an older woman who was herself struggling but still held onto God.

What overflowed from Ruth's heart was the most resplendent pledge of heart and loyalty to Naomi's God. Additionally, she displayed a faithful, unselfish devotion to her mother-in-law. What she said to Naomi is one of the most endearing things anyone could promise to another.

Naomi Wanted the Best for Ruth

Back in Bethlehem, Ruth went straight to work in order to take care of herself and Naomi. What a great daughter-in-law! By the sovereign design and kindness of the Lord, Ruth unintentionally wandered into the field of a relative named Boaz. Boaz was a kindhearted man who took notice of hard-working Ruth and then took on the support of both Ruth and Naomi. He gave Ruth extended privileges in the reaping of his fields along with extra food, extra grain, and protection.

As people do with confidantes, Ruth went home and told Naomi all about the acts of kindness that Boaz had bestowed on them. For the first time in a long time, Naomi's heavy heart lifted. She exclaimed, *"Blessed be he of the Lord, who has not forsaken his kindness to the living and the dead!"* (Ruth 2:20 NKJV). Naomi's heart, which had grown cold, was once again beginning to be encouraged by the hope and joy of God's steadfast love.

Naomi must have been elated to watch the relationship between Ruth and Boaz flourish. Who would have imagined that Naomi would once again envision a hopeful future for Ruth as a married woman? As the older, wiser woman, Naomi jumped back into her role of listening and advising and helped Ruth navigate the customs of her land for securing a husband. Naomi gave Ruth detailed instructions.

Her mother-in-law asked her, "Where did you glean today? Where did you work? Blessed be the man who took notice of you!"

Then Ruth told her mother-in-law about the one at whose place she had been working. "The name of the man I worked with today is Boaz," she said.

"The LORD bless him!" Naomi said to her daughter-in-law. "He has not stopped showing his kindness to the living and the dead." She added, "That man is our close relative; he is one of our guardian-redeemers."

Then Ruth the Moabite said, "He even said to me, 'Stay with my workers until they finish harvesting all my grain.'"

Naomi said to Ruth her daughter-in-law, "It will be good for you, my daughter, to go with the women who work for him, because in someone else's field you might be harmed."

So Ruth stayed close to the women of Boaz to glean until the barley and wheat harvests were finished. And she lived with her mother-in-law.

One day Ruth's mother-in-law Naomi said to her, "My daughter, I must find a home for you, where you will be well provided for. Now Boaz, with whose women you have worked, is a relative of ours. Tonight he will be winnowing barley on the threshing floor. Wash, put on perfume, and get dressed in your best clothes. Then go down to the threshing floor, but don't let him know you are there until he has finished eating and drinking. When he lies down, note the place where he is lying. Then go and uncover his feet and lie down. He will tell you what to do."

"I will do whatever you say," Ruth answered.
(Ruth 2:19–3:5)

Soon, Naomi had a reason for living again!

When Ruth came to her mother-in-law, Naomi asked, "How did it go, my daughter?"

Then she told her everything Boaz had done for her and added, "He gave me these six measures of barley, saying, 'Don't go back to your mother-in-law empty-handed.'"

Then Naomi said, "Wait, my daughter, until you find out what happens. For the man will not rest until the matter is settled today." (Ruth 3:16–18)

Ruth Wanted the Best for Naomi

Ruth stayed by Naomi's side even when her husband died. There was no promise of a future husband for her in this new land she was going to, but she was thinking only one thing: I will follow Naomi. Thank goodness she did not leave that old woman on the dangerous road to travel by herself. Ruth also stayed by her side because she could see the grief and bitterness in the heart of Naomi. She saw that Naomi needed her and was not critical, but caring.

Eventually, Ruth knew that Boaz could—and wanted to—provide for the aged and needy Naomi (Ruth 2:5–16; 3:17). Ruth, too, wanted that security for Naomi. Therefore, the younger woman obediently followed through on Naomi's instructions to propose marriage to Boaz. She said, *"All that you say to me I will do"* (Ruth 3:5 NKJV).

In brief, the rest of the story is every little girl's dream. At, last Ruth marries Boaz and has a baby boy whose name is Obed; he was the father of Jesse, the father of David. Ruth was part of a bigger purpose. Through Ruth would come David and then Jesus the promised Messiah!

Finally, near the end of the book of Ruth, we read

> *The women said to Naomi: "Praise be to the LORD, who this day has not left you without a guardian-redeemer. May he become famous throughout Israel! He will renew your life and sustain you in your old age. For your daughter-in-law, who loves you and who is better to you than seven sons, has given him birth."* (Ruth 4:14–15)

Naomi and Ruth offer us an exquisite illustration of selflessness. I am blessed to enjoy a few devoted friendships for life with women like Michelle Davis, Amarillis Mercado, Tracy Macaluso, Luz Martinez, Irene Rivera Rodriguez, Anne Maglore, and Yolanda Thomas. My friendship with Christina Maldonado reminds me of the friendship of Ruth and Naomi.

I will share just a few of the qualities that I believe we are blessed to have in our relationship:

Mutual Love—As Ruth and Naomi were coming from hurting places in life, they both had to decide to trust and give their hearts again. When Christina and I met, Christina certainly gave her heart, but I was not in a good place spiritually and really had to decide if I was ever going to give my heart deeply again. *"Now that you have purified yourselves by obeying the truth so that you have sincere love for each other, love one another deeply, from the heart"* (1 Peter 1:22).

Mutual Devotion—Naomi and Ruth cared for each other, supported each other, and were dedicated to each other. Although I am the "older" sister in the relationship, Christina is devoted to helping me be my best for God as well as me helping her. We are devoted to each other's families, we support each other's endeavors, and we are partners in the gospel. We are also devoted to being very gracious to each other. *"Be devoted to one another in love. Honor one another above yourselves"* (Romans 12:10).

Mutual Respect—Naomi and Ruth respected each other from the first time we meet them. Naomi could have selfishly demanded that Ruth and Orpah go with her back to Judah, but she was looking out for their best interests and respected the decisions they made. It was a very healthy relationship. In the early years of Christina's and my relationship, I as the "older" sister did most of the teaching and training yet learned tons from her. I hold her in high regard, admire her, and respect the convictions, decisions, and wisdom God has given her as an adult woman. I just want to say here to the Naomis out there that I think it's very important to let the Ruths in our lives grow up. Your relationship must evolve in order for "Ruth" to become all she is called to be.

There is no room for competition, only opportunities to bring out the best in each other. Ladies, here is a scripture that reminds us that we are all brilliantly unique and display God's splendor in different styles: *"The sun has one kind of splendor, the moon another and the stars another; and star differs from star in splendor"* (1 Corinthians 15:41).

Just as it takes a collection of many colors: red, orange, yellow, green, blue, indigo, and violet, to make a beautiful rainbow, it takes the many different qualities friends have to make a beautiful friendship, a relationship that only death can separate.

_____ DREAM DARE _____

Dare to pursue genuine relationships that help each other succeed.

For Reflection: pray...ponder...promise...practice.

Two people are better off than one, for they can help each other succeed. If one person falls, the other can reach out and help. But someone who falls alone is in real trouble. (Ecclesiastes 4:9–10 NLT)

Conclusion

Jesus Is the Greatest Dreamer Who Ever Lived

God loves to pour out His Spirit with power on those who will dare to align radically their purposes with His. —Steve Childers

I urge, then, first of all, that petitions, prayers, intercession and thanksgiving be made for all people—for kings and all those in authority, that we may live peaceful and quiet lives in all godliness and holiness. This is good, and pleases God our Savior, who wants all people to be saved and to come to a knowledge of the truth. For there is one God and one mediator between God and mankind, the man Christ Jesus, who gave himself as a ransom for all people. (1 Timothy 2:1–6a)

As we come to the finale of our experience together, I would like us to conclude in the same way we began: with our focus on God and following Jesus' example. Jesus was the greatest dreamer who ever walked the face of the earth. He accomplished God's dream for his life with the thirty-three years given him, in a human body, being tempted by every temptation known to man, yet he did not sin. This means he can relate to any and every challenge and emotion we may experience on our journey to achieve our dreams. He can also show us how to navigate life and truly succeed. Who better to look to than Jesus to obtain some practical direction and inspiration to achieve even greater things? When we study the life of Jesus, we can see that he had a purpose, a plan and passion. He picked a team, he found pleasure in his dream, and he was willing to pay the price for it. These are just a few things that we can imitate if we desire to be women who dare to dream and live out our dreams.

What Did Jesus Do? WDJD

Jesus Clearly Envisioned God's Purpose for His Life on Earth

Before I leave you, I am thrilled to share another one of my all-time favorite scriptures. To me, this scripture reveals some pertinent and motivating truths about God's will for Jesus' life and ours. Jesus proclaims himself as the One who would bring the good news to the world. This is an essential reminder to me that what Jesus brought is GOOD NEWS and we have to share it! His purpose on earth was clearly found in God's word. In Luke 3:21–23 the Bible says Jesus was baptized and began his ministry at about thirty years old. After his baptism, full of the Holy Spirit, he was led into the wilderness by that same Spirit, where he was tempted for forty days. Then in the power of the Spirit he returned to Galilee and went to Nazareth where he was brought up. There he proclaimed God's dream for his life:

He went to Nazareth, where he had been brought up, and on the Sabbath day he went into the synagogue, as was his custom. He stood up to read, and the scroll of the prophet Isaiah was handed to him. Unrolling it, he found the place where it is written:

"The Spirit of the Lord is on me,
because he has anointed me
to proclaim good news to the poor.
He has sent me to proclaim freedom for the prisoners
and recovery of sight for the blind,
to set the oppressed free,
to proclaim the year of the Lord's favor."

Then he rolled up the scroll, gave it back to the attendant and sat down. The eyes of everyone in the synagogue were fastened on him. He began by saying to them, "Today this scripture is fulfilled in your hearing." (Luke 4:16–21)

Jesus embraced the purpose for his life on earth: he would preach good news to the poor, not meaning financially destitute but indicating utter helplessness, complete destitution, and being afflicted and distressed. He would heal the brokenhearted. The Hebrew word translated "heal" means to mend (by stitching), repair thoroughly, and make whole. Jesus came to proclaim freedom for those of us who have been slaves to our sins, failures, and fears. He was sent to proclaim recovery of sight for the blind, not just physical blindness, but the spiritual blindness that keeps unbelievers from seeing the light of the gospel. He came to release the oppressed from emotional wreckage and to proclaim the year of the Lord's favor. The word translated "year" means an indefinite time. The point is that you and I are living in the year of the Lord's favor right now. We need to make the most of this opportunity while we have the chance. As 2 Corinthians 6:1–2 says,

> As God's co-workers we urge you not to receive God's grace in vain. For he says,
>> "In the time of my favor I heard you,
>> and in the day of salvation I helped you."
> I tell you, now is the time of God's favor, now is the day of salvation.

Just as Jesus' purpose in life was found in God's word, I believe that seeking God through his word and prayer will absolutely clarify what our purpose in life is. I find it very interesting that even for Jesus, there was a time and a process to undergo in order to arrive at the place of pronouncing God's dream for his life. Through his baptism and temptation, Jesus set an example for us of starting with humility and obedience to God. If you haven't committed to being a disciple of Jesus, don't be discouraged, dear friend, if it's not yet clear to you what God's dream is for your life. Just begin with pursing a relationship with God that is pleasing to him according to his word. I suggest building your relationship with God by diving into the Gospels and looking at who Jesus really is and how he lived, died and was resurrected, and who he calls us to be.

If you are a disciple and it's still not clear what God's dream is for you, don't be discouraged, my sister. Give it some time. Very often clarity comes not just in the mountaintop experiences but also in the valley, not just in the season of triumph but after a season of trials and temptation. Notice that Jesus had spent forty days being tempted in the wilderness by the devil when he made his great proclamation. Many of us have heard of Joseph the dreamer, Jacob's favorite son. When he was seventeen, he had a dream that implied that one day his brothers would bow down to him. He was a braggart about it, his brothers came to hate him, and he ended up thrown in a pit, sold into slavery, and thrown into jail before he would see the fullness of his dream come to pass. It takes time and patience to wait on God as he magnificently reveals all the interwoven pieces of his dream for us.

Moreover, I want to encourage you to take every opportunity to serve others. Remember, God chose the apostles not because they were the best and the brightest but because they were willing (Mark 3: 13–19). When you have an opportunity to serve in the church, be willing. When you are given the chance to learn something new, be willing. When circumstances take you out of your comfort zone, be willing. When you are challenged to do something you really think you won't like, be willing. Over twenty years ago, when the New York City Church of Christ kicked off the teen ministry, I was asked to train to lead teenage girls. I had no idea what I was doing, didn't think I would like teens much, and was afraid to leave the ministry in which I was serving. Today, I can't imagine my life without that experience. I found my niche, something I was good at. I fell in love with teenagers and learned so much from them. Mike would eventually join me in serving the teens, and God used Mike, me and the teens to build an amazing ministry in the Bronx. Teens are some of the most loyal people, and I am fortunate that some of those who were teens at that time are our closest friends today. I can't imagine life without those girls because they changed me forever.

When you are willing, you will be better able to hear what God's Spirit has laid on your heart. You will know what God has anointed you to do. You will live like you have been sent.

A good way to determine if something is God's dream for you is to ask yourself if it is in line with what *"pleases God our Savior, who wants all people to be saved and to come to a knowledge of the truth"* (1 Timothy 2:3–4). If your dream opposes God's dream in any way, it might turn out to be your biggest nightmare.

Jesus Picked a Team

One of those days Jesus went out to a mountainside to pray, and spent the night praying to God. When morning came, he called his disciples to him and chose twelve of them, whom he also designated apostles: Simon (whom he named Peter), his brother Andrew, James, John, Philip, Bartholomew, Matthew, Thomas, James son of Alphaeus, Simon who was called the Zealot, Judas son of James, and Judas Iscariot, who became a traitor. (Luke 6:12–16)

Jesus set an example of praying before making big decisions. He spent the whole night praying to God about who he would choose to be in his inner circle. Then he created a team of the people he needed, whom he would train to carry out his dream. If Jesus was so determined to spend time inquiring of God about his team, how much more should we be? Also, if Jesus needed a team, what does that say about us? Jesus' team was made up of unschooled, ordinary men from diverse backgrounds and with varying weaknesses, strengths, and personalities. Alone, each of them may not have seemed impressive at all, but together they changed the world.

Do you have a dream team? Have you prayed about your team? Are they people who will buy into the dream and help you to accomplish it by sharing their gifts, talents, time, and resources? Don't be discouraged if who is on your team has to change. Even Jesus had a Judas. I have to say that God has shown me favor when it comes to the incredible women's leaders' groups with whom I have served through the years. Currently I serve with a diverse team of women who excel in distinct areas of ministry. Betty Landergott is the prayer warrior, Jean Johnson and Yolanda Thomas nurture and encourage the saints, Christina Maldonado and Anne Coleman love people deeply and are keenly focused on outreach, Brunia Chisolm is a wonderful and hospitable servant, Griselda Marmolejos operates the finances with integrity, Liana Sisco is always doing good serving the poor and meeting needs in the church, Rochelle Hall is an expert event planner, and then there's always the glue, Wander Franklin. I admire these women; their strengths add so much to my life and to God's church.

Jesus Had a Plan

> *Then Jesus came to them and said, "All authority in heaven and on earth has been given to me. Therefore go and make disciples of all nations, baptizing them in the name of the Father and of the Son and of the Holy Spirit, and teaching them to obey everything I have commanded you. And surely I am with you always, to the very end of the age."* (Matthew 28:18–20)

Jesus had a plan that would supersede his physical life. His plan was his disciples. He had trained them to make disciples and teach the new disciples to obey everything he had commanded. His plan was specific, was not optional and came with a promise: I will be with you always. Honestly, by nature I am not a planner. I am more the spontaneous, let's-see-what-God-does person. For instance, when we go on vacation to the beach I like to have NO plan, just relax and decide activities as we go. I have some friends who plan the daily itinerary of their vacations months in advance. That would drive me loco. Nevertheless, because I have many close friends who are professional event planners, I have learned to appreciate them and have seen the need for making plans. As author Harvey MacKay said, "If you fail to plan, then you plan to fail."

Jesus had a plan and he worked that plan every day of his life. John 9:4–5 says, *"As long as it is day, we must do the works of him who sent me. Night is coming, when no one can work. While I am in the world, I am the light of the world."* Jesus didn't just talk about the light; he was the light. Don't just talk about it, be about it. *"All hard work brings a profit, but mere talk leads only to poverty"* (Proverbs 14:23).

Jesus Was Passionate

> He replied, "Go tell that fox, 'I will keep on driving out demons and healing people today and tomorrow, and on the third day I will reach my goal.' In any case, I must press on today and tomorrow and the next day—for surely no prophet can die outside Jerusalem!" (Luke 13:32–33)

Jesus was consumed with zeal for God's house. He was passionate about not letting Herod or the Pharisees distract him from his work and reaching Jerusalem. Jerusalem was the city of God and symbolized the entire nation. Luke 9:51 says, *"As the time approached for him to be taken up to heaven, Jesus resolutely set out for Jerusalem."* Not even sentimentality would stop him from reaching his goal. Look at Matthew 16:21–23:

> From that time on Jesus began to explain to his disciples that he must go to Jerusalem and suffer many things at the hands of the elders, the chief priests and the teachers of the law, and that he must be killed and on the third day be raised to life.
>
> Peter took him aside and began to rebuke him. "Never, Lord!" he said. "This shall never happen to you!"
>
> Jesus turned and said to Peter, "Get behind me, Satan! You are a stumbling block to me; you do not have in mind the concerns of God, but merely human concerns."

I'm challenged. I think I could be a lot more zealous, fervent, bold, and enthusiastic about my goals and dreams. How about you?

Jesus Found Pleasure in Pursuing His Dream

At that time Jesus, full of joy through the Holy Spirit, said, "I praise you, Father, Lord of heaven and earth, because you have hidden these things from the wise and learned, and revealed them to little children. Yes, Father, for this is what you were pleased to do." (Luke 10:21)

Jesus found joy is his relationship with God and in revealing himself and the Father to those he had chosen. It's always convicting to me to think of all that Jesus went through in just the three years of his ministry and yet stayed full of joy. Let's define joy: this joy is more than a feeling of happiness when all is well. The joy that Christ gives is something that no circumstance can take away. It is a quality of peace and strength that enables a believer to rejoice even amid trouble and sorrow.

Does your dream bring you pleasure? Do you enjoy pursuing it? When all is said and done, will you be pleased that you spent your precious time (the one resource you have that you can never replace) pursuing it?

_____ DREAM DARE _____

Dare to go out and pursue your dreams with joy, knowing that God will light your path as you live the dreams he has for you!

For Reflection: pray...ponder...promise...practice.

You make known to me the path of life;
  you will fill me with joy in your presence,
  with eternal pleasures at your right hand. (Psalm 16:11)

Endnotes

Introduction:
1. John C. Maxwell, *Put Your Dream to the Test: 10 Questions to Help You See It and Seize It* (Nashville, Tennessee: Thomas Nelson, 2009), 38.
2. Adapted from Holley Gerth, *You're Made for a God-Sized Dream: Opening the Door to All God Has for You*, Kindle Edition (Grand Rapids, MI: Baker Publishing Group, 2013), Kindle location 166.
3. Identity Theft Resource Center http://www.idtheftcenter.org/

Chapter 1:
1. Often attributed to Hunter S. Thompson but original source unknown.

Chapter 2:
1. Dillon Burroughs, *Hunger No More: A 1-Year Devotional Journey Through the Psalms* (Birmingham, Alabama: New Hope Publishers, 2012).
2. Munroe Myles, *Understanding the Purpose and the Power of Women: A Book for Women and the Men Who Love Them* (New Kensington, Pennsylvania: Whitaker House, 2001), 60.
3. Ibid., 81.
4. Ibid., 75.
5. Gerth, 17.
6. John MacArthur, *12 Extraordinary Women* (Nashville, Tennessee: Thomas Nelson, 2005), 242.
7. *A League of Their Own*, written by Kim Wilson, Kelly Candaele, Lowell Ganz, Babaloo Mandel.
8. Timothy Rowe, *The Magnificent Goodness of God and How It Will Transform Your Life* (Maitland, Florida: Xulon Press, 2012), 212–213.
9. *Taken*, written by Luc Besson and Robert Mark Kamen.

10. Rowe, 213.

Chapter 3
1. Gary Thomas, S*acred Marriage: What If God Designed Marriage to Make Us Holy More Than to Make Us Happy?* Kindle Edition (Grand Rapids, Michigan: Zondervan, 2008), 13, 67–68.
2. http://kidshealth.org/teen/your_mind/problems/date_rape.html#
3. http://www.heritage.org/research/reports/1997/05/bg1115-the-child-abuse-crisis, from a chart in Broken Homes and Battered Children by Robert Whelan (Family Education Trust, 1994)
4. http://www.confidencecoalition.org/statistics-women

Chapter 4
1. "Quilt of Life" by Fern Estes, Golden Poet of the Year Award 1987

Chapter 5
1. Elizabeth George, *Discovering the Treasures of a Godly Woman: Proverbs 31,* Kindle Edition (Eugene, Oregon: Harvest, 2003), Kindle locations 293–294.
2. George, *Beautiful in God's Eyes: The Treasures of the Proverbs 31 Woman* (Eugene, Oregon: Harvest House, 1998).
3. George, *Discovering the Treasures of a Godly Woman,* Kindle location 333.
4. "Independent Women" written by Beyoncé Knowles, Sam Barnes, Jean-Claude Olivier and Cory Rooney, 2000.
5. George, *Discovering the Treasures of a Godly Woman,* Kindle location 334.
6. Thomas, 33.

Chapter 6
1. www.cdc.gov/violenceprevention/pub/youth_suicide.html

Chapter 7
1. http://lexiconcordance.com/hebrew/7665.html
2. http://www.mayoclinic.com/health/broken-heart-syndrome/DS01135

Chapter 8
1. Douglas Jacoby, *The Spirit: The Work of the Holy Spirit in the Lives of Disciples* (Spring, Texas: Illumination Publishers International, 1998, 2005), 55.

Chapter 9

1. Joyce Meyer, *Straight Talk on Loneliness: Overcoming Emotional Battles with the Power of God's Word!* Kindle Edition (Denver, Colorado: Faithworks, 2009), Kindle location 139.
2. Ibid., Kindle locations 139–140.
3. Ibid., Kindle locations 125–127.
4. Ashley Schnarr, *Single Girl: The Single Woman's Guide to Life, Liberty And the Pursuit of Godliness*, Kindle Edition (www.ashleyschnarr.com, 2013), Kindle location 219.
5. Ibid., Kindle location 273.
6. George Madison Adams (1837–1920), U.S. Representative from Kentucky.

Chapter 10

1. http://storify.com/lifeclass/oprah-and-iyanla-vanzant-single-mothers-raising-so
2. Ann Spangler and Jean E. Syswerda, *Women of the Bible: A One-Year Devotional Study of Women in Scripture* (Grand Rapids, Michigan: Zondervan, 2006), 34.
3. Ibid., 33
4. Ibid., 33

Chapter 12

1. *Life Application Study Bible NIV, Revised* (Carol Stream, Illinois: Tyndale House Publishers, 1983), 750.
2. Dee Brestin, *A Woman of Faith, Esther: Overcoming the World's Influences* (Elgin Illinois: NexGen, Cook Communications Ministries, 2006), 15–16.
3. Dele Oke, "Esther - Women of the Bible" http://www.wordlibrary.co.uk/article.php?id=159.
4. Brestin, 36.

Chapter 13

1. Douglas Jacoby, *The Spirit: The Work of the Holy Spirit in the Lives of Disciples* (Spring, Texas: Illumination Publishers International, 1998, 2005), 51–57.
2. *Life Application Study Bible NIV, Revised* (Carol Stream, Illinois: Tyndale House Publishers, 1983), 1847.

3. Ann Spangler and Jean E. Syswerda, *Women of the Bible: A One-Year Devotional Study of Women in Scripture* (Grand Rapids, Michigan: Zondervan, 2006), 405.

Chapter 15

1. Brenda Poinsett, *She Walked with Jesus: Stories of Christ Followers in the Bible* (Birmingham, Alabama: New Hope Publishers, 2004), 132.
2. Ibid. 130
3. Ibid. 133

Chapter 16

1. *Theological Dictionary of the Old Testament*, Volume 7, eds. G. Botterweck, H. Ringgren, H. Fabry (Grand Rapids, Michigan: Wm. B. Eerdmans, 1984), 166. Due to the importance of having an heir, in the Hebrew culture there was no substantial difference between a bride and any married woman or widow without children.

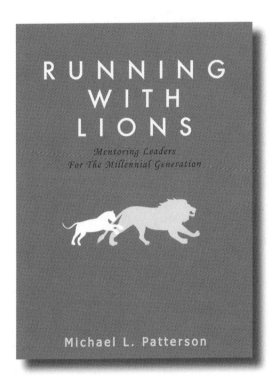

Michael L. Patterson is an evangelist, author, and adjunct professor. With over two decades of experience in church leadership, Michael has mentored and trained many leaders who serve all over North America. He holds a master's of Science in History from Florida State University and has taught at the prestigious Morehouse College in Atlanta, Georgia. He currently serves as lead evangelist of the Greater Atlanta Church of Christ. Michael may be contacted at: TheGACC@gmail.com.

Available at www.ipibooks.com

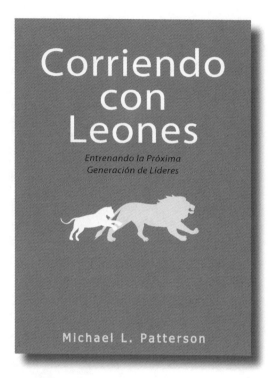

Acerca del autor: **Michael L. Patterson** es evangelista, autor y profesor adjunto. Con más de veinte años de experiencia dirigiendo Iglesias, Michael ha aconsejado y entrenado varios líderes que ahora sirven en toda América del Norte. Él tiene una maestría en Historia de la Florida State University y ha enseñado en la prestigiosa universidad Morehouse College en Atlanta, Georgia. Él es el evangelista principal de la Iglesia de Cristo de Atlanta (Greater Atlanta Church of Christ). Para comunicarse con Michael puede escribirle al e-mail: TheGACC@gmail.com.

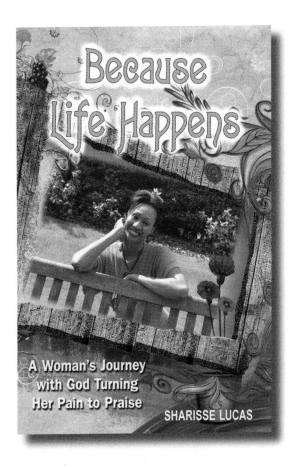

About the author: Currently on the mission field in the United Kingdom, Sharisse Lucas has been a Christian for twenty-three years, eighteen of them in full-time ministry serving families, teens, campus and singles in L.A., Dallas, Houston, the UK and Boston. She has been a keynote speaker for numerous inspirational women's functions in the United States as well as Belize, Mexico, London and Paris. She and her husband, Marvin, have been married for twenty-one years and have two children ages thirteen and ten. Sharisse has also been a runway, commercial and print model for over twenty years on the East and West coasts and in Europe, with such clients as Pepsi, New Balance and Reebok and has owned a model consulting business.

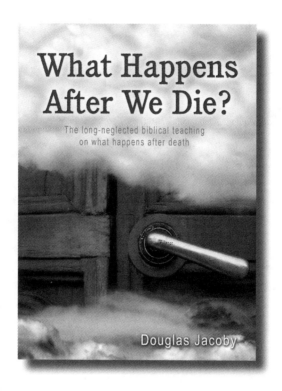

Dr. Douglas Jacoby graduated in 1980 from Duke University (history). In 1982, he received an MTS from Harvard (New Testament), followed by three years of post-graduate study at Kings College London. He took his doctorate from Drew University. Douglas has had an international teaching impact, preaching in 500 cities in over 100 nations. He also serves as professor of Bible and theology at Lincoln Christian University. For additional information about his work and ministry, visit www.DouglasJacoby.com and www.jacobypremium.com.

www.ipibooks.com